DEAR MIDOL:
ESSAYS FROM ESTROGEN HELL

CONTENTS

ACKNOWLEDGMENTS

Parenting is expensive.
My wife is a saint.
Cats are annoying.
I like fudge.

PREFACE

Like everything worthwhile in my life, the genesis of this book came from my wife, Ellen.

Back in 1990, we had just moved from Indianapolis to Birmingham, Alabama, with our three young daughters. Smack dab in the middle of the Deep South, we were far away from friends and family, far away from our support system of parents and sister baby-sitters, far away from anyone who had never eaten possum.

So, as a way to keep up with everyone up north, Ellen had the bright idea to write the much-dreaded family Christmas letter.

There is nothing I hated more than that annual bragathon of one-upmanship.

> Dear Friends Whose Lives Are Miserable:
> As we prepare for our annual ski trip—we have found the most divine private ski lodge in the town of Engelberg in the Swiss Alps, far away from the chance of ever bumping into the likes of you— we want to pause once again to remind ourselves about the true meaning of Christmas: being able to wipe our asses with your miserable lives.

Once again, our bright and shiny kids are the brightest and shiniest in their bright, shiny private school. They are out of rehab and doing well.

Jim is now a full partner in his firm and, with the embarrassment of perks coming our way, we just bought a multimillion-dollar mansion. Perhaps we will not have you over if you're ever in the area.

In June, I had a second breast implant surgery. This time, on my back. So, now I can work two stages in the club at once. Oh, the money I am making!

Anyway, the Alps are calling, so I must run. We will gloat at you miserable losers next year.

Merry Christmas

The Assholetons, Jim and Mimi

"Nah, forget that," I told Ellen. "I hate those things."

Being a female, she continued browbeating me to write one. Finally, in a moment of weakness and Jack Danielsness, I agreed.

"OK, I'll do it, but I will not write a rosy-cheeked letter about how great our lives are. For God's sake, we have three daughters who might be functionally insane, I write advertising for a living, and we live in Birmingdamn, Alabama. I will write about that. If you have a problem with it, write it yourself."

After all, parenthood isn't a Christmas postcard. Parenthood is Munch's *The Scream*. Parenthood isn't unicorn tears and vanilla-scented elf farts. Parenthood is a throbbing hangnail.

Recognizing that writing it herself would require an output of energy on her part, she agreed.

So, in the winter of 1992, I wrote our first Sutton family Christmas letter. It talked about hitting our kids over the head with a baseball bat, gutting cats, and other traditional family holiday topics.

Most people thought it was funny. So, I wrote another one the following year. Friends and family continued taking our calls, so I continued writing them.

Eventually, Ellen and I moved to Texas and had two more daughters. As the five girls grew into women, and thoughts of faking my own death grew exponentially with them, each Christmas letter became less an actual letter and more a desperate cry for help.

Just how offensive could I get in a Christmas letter? What topics are off limits? How far is too far? Would I say something that would upset my mom?

Surprisingly, those questions never entered my mind.

So, I wrote about the pleasantries of bitch slapping and cat pee and vasectomies and more cat pee and the various stages of having my testicles in a vise.

And people seemed to like it. Year after year, we'd get calls from friends and family telling us how much they looked forward to our Christmas letters, and how every year they would gather around the tree to read our Christmas letter aloud to their families (who are no doubt drunk).

My misery had become a holiday tradition.

Next, they started saying things like, "You ought to put your Christmas letters in a book."

So, I got to thinking, *Maybe I ought to.* But then it occurred to me that nobody is going to pay eighty-nine dollars for a book with a few stupid Christmas letters from some stupid family from Dallas. I will need to fill it up with other meaningful crap.

What follows is a collection of our family holiday letters (they start out slow but, trust me, they get better), along with essays on parenthood, manhood, raising daughters, navigating a wife, baseball, and helpful tips on shaving one's ball sack.

Cleverly disguised as a letter to the fine makers of Midol, this book is in fact a male self-help guide, a cautionary tale, and an accurate account of the joys, the sorrows, and the discarded panty liners that come from having a wife and five daughters.

It's a portrait of an American family.

Some things I wrote about might be too offensive. Some things might be off limits. Some things might go too far. Some things might upset my mom.

But, that never occurred to me until now, and the book is pretty much already written.

So, thank you for reading *Dear Midol:*. I hope you enjoy one man's desperate plea for normalcy in a world of estrogen, times six.

Thank you for buying it as well.

And congratulations, your check cleared.

A HEARTFELT APOLOGY

Before I go any further, I would like to apologize.

I am truly sorry to all individuals concerned whom I will have offended in the near or distant future with my humor, razor-sharp wit, and musings on living with women.

Please forgive me for what I am going to be saying or doing in the future that you will find offensive. After I commit that offensive statement or action, I will be working hard on being a better person. With my family at my side, I will announce that it will not have been my intention to insult you, nor will it have been my intention to make you cry like the way-too-sensitive baby you obviously are. Are you too fragile to take a joke? Apparently so. I will not have known that at the time.

While it will soon be clear that you never developed thick skin, I should have had the foresight to recognize you do not possess the faculties to sustain having your shortcomings, such a long list as it is, pointed out to you.

You will most certainly be appalled at my callous or cavalier attitude toward your feelings, however overreactionary and totally meritless your alleged insults may be. For that I will be deeply sorry.

I am not sure how long you have been humorless and void of the ability to laugh at yourself or to recognize your misgivings—most certainly with all the misgivings you possess, what I will say to offend you cannot be the first time such an occurrence occurred—but the term "grow a pair" will come to my mind during this ordeal. Sorry for that as well. But, come on, grow a pair.

In the ensuing media frenzy attacking my character, I will refrain from verbalizing that you are a pantywaist, a wimp, a creampuff, a pussy, a lightweight, a Penn State trustee, or anything else that might imply you are one nut shy of Lance Armstrong.

Please accept my apology.

DEAR MIDOL:
ESSAYS FROM ESTROGEN HELL

A PLEA FOR HELP, A JOB APPLICATION

Dear Midol:

 I have a wife and five daughters. You make a PMS pill. We need to talk.

 I'm sure you are very proud of your product. And I'm sure you are very proud of your company's advances in the field of menstruation sciences.

 I bet you are even very proud of your Research and Development Department over there in Ovulation Station, or whatever fancy name you have for your corporate campus.

 But here's the deal. I'm not impressed.

 If the guys in R&D were really actually guys, they would have figured out long ago that there is a gaping hole (sorry, poor choice of words) in your product offering.

 You see, while your fine product covers one week of the month, has it ever occurred to anyone over there that a month has four weeks? What the hell are men supposed to do the other three weeks?

 Fortunately, I can help you out there. I have a lifetime of intensive research living with and among women (and for the first nine months of my existence, actually inside one). I am willing to share with you my findings.

Consider this book a job application. I want to run your R&D Department.

Let me rephrase that. You *need* me to run your R&D Department.

Allow me to rephrase once more. For the good of humanity, America, and the resolve of our allies overseas, I *absolutely must* run your R&D Department.

No human being is better suited at understanding women than I am. And while I still have my last shards of sanity, I am sharing those insights with you throughout the following pages. Insights that will benefit not just your company, but men and fathers everywhere will find my findings invaluable.

Oh, the things I could tell you. I could write a book.

DO NOT BE A LAZY ASSHOLE DICKHEAD

One day my wife, Ellen, and I had a daughter. We named her Beth. Even though she was born without a penis, we loved her just the same.

But, being a guy, I thought, *It sure would be nice to have a son.* So, a few years later we figured we'd give it a whirl. That whirl gave us two more daughters. Twins. Julie and Kelly.

Soon a fourth daughter came. Caroline. Then a fifth daughter. Running out of names, we stuck Katie on her.

Four tries. Five daughters. The Sperm Fairy has a wicked sense of humor.

So there I was. Stranded in Estrogen Hell. A wife and five daughters. And me.

This book is filled with real-life advice on living with women, on being a father, on parenthood. This book is filled with lots of misery.

Even though I have five daughters, I am not going to be so foolish as to tell you I am an expert on having children, or on raising girls. All I can do is share my experiences with you.

Anyone who tells you that he is an expert at child rearing is, in my book (and, hey, this is my book!), lying. It's all a crapshoot, despite the sage advice and expertise of the so-called experts. Look on the jacket of every book written by a supposed parenting expert and you will read the same thing: "Lives alone in Malibu with sixteen cats."

Parenting doesn't even work the same within the same family. How many seemingly normal, well-adjusted people do you know who have a sibling who is Britney-Spears-to-the-power-of-Charlie-Sheen crazy?

Same parents. Same DNA. Same upbringing. One normal, the other bat-shit nuts.

Nobody knows anything. Best you can do if you are a father of daughters is to raise them to stay off the pole and hope that the fathers of sons raise their boys not to be the guys tossing dollars at the girls on the pole.

Parenthood is all about, when it boils down to it, controlling what goes into them and what comes out of them. Simple as that.

What comes out are bodily fluids and words and thoughts and hissy fits and kids. What goes in are food and medicine and thoughts and mind-altering things that can screw up those thoughts.

When they are little, though, what mostly comes out of them is pee, crap, vomit, and snot. Your life from the time they are born until the time they are about ten will be a Thomas Edison-like adventure of trying to invent ways to get their pee, crap, vomit, and snot from Point A (which is every one of their blowholes) to Point B (the closest toilet, bathroom, or State of West Virginia border) without getting any on your shirt, your hair, your shoes, or between your fingers.

Good luck.

And when I say snot, I am talking lots of snot. My scientific research has shown that a human child can generate nineteen thousand times its body weight per day in snot. So much snot, in fact, that some childless child expert invented a thing called the nasal aspirator. The snot sucker. It's a rubber device with a tapered funnel-like tube on one end and a squeeze ball on the other end.

You're supposed to stick that rubber tube up the kid's nose and pump the ball, forming a vacuum that extracts snot out of the nose, through the tube and into the rubber ball.

Good luck with that. Babies love lying still while you stick things in them.

But let's assume you are successful at sucking out the snot from your baby's nose. Then what?

The cat-loving genius who invented this genius invention stopped there. He didn't say what to do afterward.

What the hell is one supposed to do with a snot-filled rubber ball of snot? The EPA won't let you throw them away. So, like with half-empty cans of paint, you're forced to find a shelf in the garage and stack up your rubber snot balls, one by one, and hope you don't run out of room.

It takes about a month and a half to amass enough rubber snot balls to fill an average two-car garage.

Then what?

My best advice is to do what I have done. Go down to the local park and toss them to dogs. People who have a Saturday to spend at the park with their dogs have no children. Which means, they have no idea what a nasal aspirator is.

They are grateful as hell for the crazy-eyed man at the park passing out free rubber chew toys to their dogs.

They have no idea that the snot seeping out all over their dog came out of my daughter about four years ago and has since been fermenting in that snot holder in my hot garage all this time. They just see their dog having the time of its life chewing on a funny-shaped rubber chew toy ball thing.

Luckily, dog snot looks very much like kid snot. Thank you, God, for that one.

As far as controlling what else comes out of them, like words and thoughts and personalities, my best advice to guys is this:

Do not, under any circumstances, think that as a man parenthood is only a woman's job. That is your kid there, buddy. That is your responsibility. You are either the laziest asshole alive or the biggest dickhead in the world if you expect your wife to do all the work.

Do you know how long it takes to change a diaper? About a minute. Do you know how long it takes to erase the mantle of being a lazy asshole dickhead? Your entire life.

I've always had a huge problem with the selfishness of guys who think it's the woman's job to cook, rear children, clean, do laundry. Why didn't you just marry your mom?

You should not still be breast-feeding on your own mom when your kids are breast-feeding on theirs.

Parenting isn't a chore that gets in the way. Parenting is the single greatest thing that could ever happen to you. Yeah, it's a pain in the ass a lot of times. Some days, even most of the time. But so are you, and most people let you live.

Dads who tell me, "Sorry, can't go out tonight, I have to baby-sit the kids," make me sad. Not that they can't go out, but because they look at parenting as a chore. I always ask them, "Wow, what is your wife paying you to baby-sit, two bucks an hour? Do you get pizza rolls?"

She's probably out with a man who doesn't think parenting is baby-sitting.

There is not a better feeling in the world than coming home from work and hanging out with your kids. At the office, all day long, you are told you suck—by your bosses, by your co-workers, by your clients. You dropped the ball on this and that. You are a disgrace to the company, the industry, and the economy. Oh, and you need to wear pants to the office from now on.

No matter how rotten your day goes, it all vanishes the moment you walk into your house. In an instant you go from being Tom Cruise to being Tom Hanks.

For some reason, when they are little, your kids love you unconditionally. You open that door and they are, like, "Yippee, there's that older gentleman again! He's back! Yeah! He's going to take me to the park and push me on that swing and toss me in the air and make me laugh! Welcome home, older gentleman! I've been waiting for you! Oh, and I think I have a hunk of crap lodged in my diaper you might want to check on."

You walking in that door is truly the happiest moment in their day. How cool is that?

It's not a matter of being your kid's friend (which is mostly a bad idea—think about it, your friends are the ones who talked you into lighting the homecoming float on fire; do you really need a junior arsonist running around waiting until you go to sleep so she can set fire to your plasma TV?). It's really a matter of being there for them. That's all. Just care.

It's amazing how much pure joy you can get out of those little shitting machines in those rare moments when they are not shitting.

I know guys who are forty-five years old and don't know how to make a bed. I know guys who brag they never once changed a diaper. I know guys who don't know how to run an iron.

That's not a badge of pride. To me, that's a sign with neon letters that reads: "I AM A LAZY IRRESPONSIBLE DICKHEAD WHO EXPECTS EVERYTHING TO BE HANDED TO ME."

It's your kid. Be a man. Raise it.

Men are pretty damn good at it, too. When a dad is actively involved in child rearing, kids ends up better. Much smarter, more grounded, more self-assured.

Am I saying men are better at raising kids than women? I would never presume to say such a ludicrous statement like that (such a thing would totally end my chances of ever reentering the vaginal pleasure zone).

What I am saying is—and this has been proven in countless books written by countless people who live alone with countless cats—that when the father is actively involved in child rearing, children have better social development, higher self-esteem, higher grades, and do better later in life.

Dads make better kids. Better kids make better adults. Better adults make better drinking buddies.

You know that asshole at the end of the bar wearing the Ed Hardy shirt and the Zubaz pants with the itchy trigger finger, just waiting for someone to look at him so he can say, "What are you looking at?" and you try to avoid confrontation so you casually respond, "Nothing," and he takes that as a personal affront and barks out, "So are you calling me nothing?" and he wants to fight you and your friends right there on the spot? That guy had a crappy dad.

Ignore your daughters and they will come back later with redneck boyfriends to kick your ass in a bar fight.

You know how Pythagoras is always going around town shooting off his mouth about "his" right triangle theorem when Babylonian mathematicians played around with it centuries before? Well, in the same way, women are always hogging the credit for successful child rearing, when in reality, men play as important a role.

When it comes to raising girls, there is not a single greater influence in a woman's life than the relationship she has with her father. It is a deep, lasting relationship that will dictate how she deals with her boyfriends, her husband, her boss, her co-workers, even her sons.

I hear women who are dating say this a lot: "All men are such jerks." I usually tell them, "That's not true. Maybe it's just that all men are jerks to you."

Don't let your daughter be a jerk magnet. You want your daughter to marry into an abusive relationship? Easy. Be the kind of dad who drinks a lot, slaps his wife around, rarely comes home, chases any skirt that moves, and never once would consider taking an interest in anything the kid does at school. It's your call.

I honestly cannot understand how any dad cannot take an active role in his kid's life. Even if you have absolutely no idea what the hell you are doing, you can be a good dad. Just hang out. Bounce a ball. Prop up a doll during a tea party. Let them color you with lipstick while you sleep. It's minimal effort for maximum results.

Hey, even if you are a cheap ass, being a good dad makes good financial sense. You want to pay for the fewest weddings as possible. Raise your daughters right and you will save a shitload on weddings.

So, to summarize: don't be a lazy asshole dickhead.

MEANWHILE, HERE ON EARTH

One of the most popular books on living with women is John Gray's *Men Are from Mars, Women Are from Venus.*

If only.

How great would that be? As she is starting in on you about cleaning out the attic or fixing the sulfuric acid carbon dioxide hydra-filter that's on the fritz and that you promised you'd fix last night, which in Venus time was about 117 Earth days ago, she looks up to see you hightailing it out on your intergalactic scooter, heading off to a great night of poker and beer with the guys on Mars. You're, like, "Glad that shit's two hundred seventeen million miles behind me."

The problem is, men are from Earth and women are from Earth. We share the same litter box.

That is the wisdom I am trying to impart here. Earth-to-Earth interactions. Mainly, how to live with women. How to raise women.

As much as I tried to raise my daughters to possess reason and logic and common sense, I was very careful not to cross the gender line and raise them as boys. I got as close to the line as I could, then tapped the brakes.

There is a trend among some ultra-progressive parents to insist gender roles be eliminated and let boys wear skirts and play with dolls and take up quilting as a hobby if that's what they want (in almost every story you read about this, for some reason, it's the boys who are allowed to be raised as girls, not vice versa).

Kids are not a social experiment. Check back on those boys in eighteen years. They will be easy to pick out of a crowd. They will be the ones with the penises in their mouths.

There is nothing wrong with that, of course. But they will have penises in their mouths nonetheless.

(On a side note, I don't get why there is such fervor in America over legalizing gay marriages. If that's what two adults want to do, go for it. But the question is, why the heck would you want to subject yourself to that brand of hell if you don't have to? You have the most ironclad excuse in the world. "Sorry, Steve, I'd marry you and spend the rest of my life ruing that decision and desperately dreaming of the day Tom Cruise comes into the Restoration Hardware and sweeps me off my feet, but it's against the law." Most heterosexual men would sign up for that deal in a heartbeat.)

Gender relations may be clear cut on Mars and Venus, but on Earth they are getting harder and harder to define—mainly because people are trying so desperately to define them in the first place. Hey, you mess with the natural order of things, you get burned.

In the fall of 2012, IKEA, the Swedish company valued for its ultra-advanced views and eco-sensitive, gender-political social progressiveness, got itself into serious hot water by trying to be gender sensitive, but failing miserably.

IKEA prints a catalog. It's a big deal. It generates billions of dollars for the company.

One day IKEA decided it was going to expand into the Arab market. (Who knew there was a market for ready-toassemble bombproof coffee tables and shelving?) But someone in the company, who obviously held the title of vice president, ran across some marketing research that women are second-class citizens in Saudi Arabia. So IKEA did what any forward-thinking, socially progressive company would do. It chose profits over consciousness.

IKEA took the exact catalog it sent all over the world and airbrushed out all those pig infidel females. Women have no place in Saudi society and, apparently, in their furniture catalogs.

Even the Swedish trade minister admonished IKEA for it, saying, "You can't delete women from society."

As much as you might like to at times, you cannot send them in a pneumatic tube to Venus. You have to deal with them here. Mostly, it's a head scratcher.

Take a look at how your wife interacts with women when she is pregnant and you will understand what I am talking about.

A woman who is a total stranger will come up to your wife and say, "So, when are you due? Is your cervix dilating? How is your vagina holding up? Are you still secreting menstrual fluid? Are you going to breast-feed? What's your nipple management strategy? I remember when my water broke. Here, let me show you, I kept it in a jar in my purse. No, that's not pickle juice, that's my amniotic fluid."

Without even the least bit of shame or hesitation, some woman your wife has never met begins asking her the most personal of questions about her body. Asking about places you yourself have never even been.

They will chat like long-lost friends, swap the most intimate personal details and stories, even have charts and graphs they had prepared for times like this.

Imagine if men did that. "Hey, stranger, got any discharge coming out of your penis hole?"

Earthlings.

THE DIFFERENCE BETWEEN CATS AND DOGS

I've heard of guys buying their wives things like irons for their birthdays. Or giving them vacuum cleaners for Valentine's Day. And while I admire their sense of pragmatism—I mean, if she needs an iron and you have to blow money on her anyway, why waste it on another worthless damn necklace that, I swear, will not flatten one single inch of wrinkled cotton?—I am ashamed, as a man, for their sense of shortsightedness.

No matter how badly a woman needs an iron (hell, she might even iron clothes for a living or be a topless lingerie iron model, in which case you get her everything ever sold), you never, ever, ever get her an iron as a gift.

Even if she asks for an iron, I promise you she will never forgive you for it, and you will regret it for the rest of your life that you will suddenly wish ended soon.

It's funny. Because women have absolutely no qualms about getting a guy, say, a drill or a cordless screwdriver as a gift. And, really, what's the difference?

Give a woman an iron and it's basically saying, "Here you go. This will help you in completing your menial household chore much better and more efficiently than that subpar ironing you were doing before." And for your act of kindness and honesty, they get really, really offended.

But when a woman gives a guy a drill, isn't she pretty much saying the same thing? "Here you go. This will help you in completing your menial household drilling tasks much better and more efficiently now than that subpar drilling you were doing. Chuck down the street is a much better driller."

Hey, drilling shit isn't fun. Guys don't get together for a night of drinking and drilling shit. Drilling shit is labor. Ironing shit is labor.

But, yes, there is a difference between a man buying a woman an iron for her birthday and a woman buying a man a drill for his birthday.

It's called Having a Vagina.

Logic and reason and common sense and even more logic get sucked up into that thing and, no matter how much you poke around in there, you won't find it.

One day when my twins were in seventh grade, Ellen asked me to run to the pet store to buy some cat food. (I have discovered to my dismay that if you feed those things, it will just encourage them to live.)

I took Julie with me and we went to PetSmart, where they were hosting Pick a Pal dog adoptions.

These people are geniuses. They have a product (dogs), they know their target audience (dog lovers), and they know exactly how to reach that target audience (pet stores). It's like when the Southern Baptist preachers convention comes to town, the hookers don't hang out at the Home Depot. They go to the lobby of the hotel where the preachers are staying. Know your target audience.

That particular day, when Julie and I went in for cat food, we came out with a black Lab puppy.

As we're leaving, Julie asked me the question she, as a female, is legally mandated to ask, "Is Mom going to be OK with us bringing home a dog?"

I recounted a story to her. "Julie, when your mom and I first got married, before we had any kids, we lived in a tiny apartment in Indianapolis. One day I got home, and guess what? Your mom had gotten a cat. She knew I hated cats. She knew if she would have discussed it with me beforehand, I would have said, 'Absolutely no.' So, without asking, she brought home a cat. Now, Julie, I have to admit I was pretty mad about that. But your mom just laughed it off and said, 'I wanted a cat.' And that was that. End of argument. Then, about three months later, she decided that *that* cat needed a cat friend. Suddenly, we became a two-cat household. So, to answer your question, Julie, in light of that story, I don't see why your mom would have a problem with me bringing home a dog. She is a fan of the surprise pet."

"YOU BROUGHT HOME A WHAT? A DOG? WHO TOLD YOU THAT YOU COULD BRING HOME A DOG? HOW COULD YOU DO SOMETHING LIKE THAT WITHOUT ASKING ME FIRST? HOW DARE YOU?"

Logic. Reason. Common sense. And even more logic. Vanished somewhere in the black hole of womanhood.

"Wait," I asked, "how is this any different than when you brought home Frankie, and then three months later you decided Frankie needed a cat buddy and next thing I knew, you brought home Johnnie? How is that any different?"

"IT IS TOTALLY DIFFERENT."

"Ah, I don't really see how."

"ARE YOU BLIND? ONE IS A CAT. THE OTHER IS A DOG. YOU DON'T KNOW THE DIFFERENCE BETWEEN A CAT AND A DOG?"

Yes, I know the difference between a cat and a dog.

It's called Having a Vagina.

1992

If hitting the kids over the head with a baseball bat won't slow them down, nothing will.

The year 1992 started out inauspiciously enough in the Sutton household. Beth was in her first year of kindergarten. Ellen was in her first year at Protective Life. Kevin was in his third year at his company. And the twins, Julie and Kelly, were in…well, they were just into everything. Then it snowed one Sunday in January. People were dumbfounded. Snow is as foreign to Birmingham as a Martin Luther King Jr. memorial. When it finished, seven inches were on the ground. Birmingham's worst snowstorm in forty years. The next day it was sixty-five degrees. By Tuesday all the snow had melted. By February, Ellen got a new job at the phone company (she won't answer the phone at home anymore, says it's too much like work). In March, the twins turned three, apiece. In April, Beth started her second year of Little League. She was involved in the most memorable play of the year. While playing second base, the batter hit a ball to her, but she was turned around talking to the outfielder, so the ball hit her in the butt and ricocheted to our first baseman, who got the runner out at first. Beth's butt was credited with an assist. Ellen's butt was credited with Beth, Julie, and Kelly. In May, Beth moved on from playing T-ball to playing barber. She cut every hair off the top of Julie's head, except for three scraggly little follicles. She was in the process of turning Kelly into a female Sinead O'Connor when Ellen caught her. Beth was so proud of her sisters, saying, "They sat real still for me, Mommy, and let me cut their hair." A look of joy failed to cross Ellen's face. In June, while Beth was playing baseball, Kelly was playing in the playground at the ballpark, where some odd kid was swinging a baseball bat for some odd reason. Unfortunately for Kelly, he swung it right into her forehead. She fell flat on the ground, motionless, and it was pretty scary for a few minutes. The ambulance and paramedics had to take her to the hospital. She got six stitches in her head, at her hairline (luckily it missed her right eye), and her eye got dark purple and swelled up so much that it stuck out about three inches further than her nose. On the bright side, though, it was finally easy to tell Julie and Kelly apart. "Oh, Julie's the one who looks like a badass skinhead. Kelly's the one who looks like a bad prizefighter." A woman at the mall told Kevin that social services should go to his house and investigate his family. He told her it was a good thing he kept the rest of his kids in the trunk of his car so they couldn't find them at home. Even with stitches in her head, Kelly went at full speed, running smack into a big glass wall at the mall, falling down, and crying out, "I thought it was the outside," and giving herself a matching bruise on the left side of her face. Fortunately, Kelly recovered beautifully, she gained fond memories of her ride in the "am-blee-ance," and the people at the ballpark bought her a stuffed bear from their Who-Needs-Litigation? collection. And Julie got a new nickname out of the whole ordeal: Coconut, as a result of her uncanny resemblance, sans hair. The same night Kelly got hit in the head, Molly (the cat) had four kittens, which were gotten rid of quickly. Anyway, the summer passed, Beth turned six and, in August, started first grade. In October, Ellen took up the violin after a fourteen-year hiatus. Kevin noted that if she would have taken it up in June, they could have saved some real money on strings, as catgut was in abundant supply. Anyway, that pretty much brings us up to the present. Ellen told Kevin she wants to have another kid. Kevin does too, but he can't find anyone to trade, so it looks like they're stuck with the ones they have. And now Christmas is upon us and we can only wish one thing: God, it had better not snow in Birmingham next year.

Merry Christmas from Kevin and Ellen and Beth and Julie and Kelly Sutton.

1993

The year of the blizzard, the day of the gizzard, the kiss of the lizard.

It started out normally enough in the Sutton household, this year called 1993. In fact, it arrived on January 1, just as expected. Sometime shortly after that, though, things got a little weird. In March, on the day Kevin left for New Orleans on business, Birmingham had its second freak snowstorm in two years. The average yearly snowfall in Birmingham is half an inch. That night, we got seventeen inches. You know it's a lot of snow when even people in Birmingham complain it's too white around here. Needless to say, the Birmingham airport was closed and Kevin was stuck in New Orleans for five days. (All in all, not a bad place to be stranded.) Ellen's parents, who were driving on their way to Florida and decided to make a quick stop to say hi, ended up being stranded for four days. You've heard of long good-byes. This was a long, long hello. The kids built snowmen, had snowball fights, went sledding, and generally had the time of their lives with their grandparents, who haven't been back since. In April, Kevin went on a tour of a chicken processing plant for work. On that day, a number of clichés were either proven or debunked. For instance, contrary to popular belief, chickens don't run around wild when their heads get cut off, at least not if they're hanging upside down by their little chicken ankles. On the other hand, it was proven that you cannot, indeed, count your chickens before they hatch. All in all, it was a strange experience. And Kevin would like to pass along this piece of advice: never, never, never, never, never, never, never, never, never, never, never, never, ever eat a hot dog. That's where many of the unhatched, and detached, chickens end up. In May, Beth lost her first tooth. Kevin told her she'd get a quarter from the Tooth Fairy. She informed him that nowadays it's a dollar. Apparently, the Tooth Fairies' union had a very successful bargaining year. In June, Kevin and Ellen had their ten-year anniversary. They celebrated by going to Bermuda for a week. Unbelievable as it sounds, some friends actually volunteered to keep the kids that week. (They haven't returned our phone calls since, though.) In August, Ellen played violin in a production of *The King and I*. But, being in the south, they changed it slightly to *Me 'n' Elvis 'n' Them*. In September, Kevin went to Mexico and saw his first bullfight in Tijuana. They actually kill the bulls. It was the most disgusting thing he'd ever paid money to see (the trip to Bourbon Street in New Orleans was a close second, though). If, however, they were to use cats instead of bulls, Kevin would be a season-ticket holder. Beth started playing basketball this year. The concept of dribbling has her baffled, though. She needs to quit watching game film of the NBA. Julie and Kelly started T-ball this summer. Kevin was the coach. They liked to bat, they liked to run the bases, they liked to sit in the dugout, they liked to go to the bathroom between innings (in fact, they led the league in RBIs, Restroom Breaks per Inning), they liked going to the concession stand after games, they liked wearing their uniforms (or what Kelly called their "costumes"), they liked to slide into the bases, they liked to spit, they liked to scratch themselves. They hated to play in the outfield. One day, during a game, while lying down in right field, Kelly called out, "Daddy, can I play in the dirt?" He said, "I think you're too young to play infield." She replied, "Who cares about that? I'm talking about the dirt pile behind the fence." She has really taken to the game. Life with Beth and Julie and Kelly is never dull. It's never quiet. But it's never dull. One day we gave Beth a piece of candy and she said, "Are you gambling with my health?" What's she going to say when she gets her first beer next year? The twins found two chameleons outside. They quickly became pets. Daisy and Rainbow. Every night we'd find moths and worms and throw them into the chameleon cage and watch them get eaten. It was the Alabama version of a dinner show. Before we left for Indianapolis for Thanksgiving, we decided we'd let the chameleons go, fearing that they'd die without food and water for days (that logic actually worked on them). Julie understood, but was sad. As she was letting Daisy go, she decided to give her a good-bye kiss. Daisy must have thought Julie's lip looked like one of the worms she'd been snacking on, and the next thing Ellen saw was Julie screaming at the top of her lungs with a chameleon dangling off her lip like a lounge singer's cigarette. It took a good minute to pry it off her lip. It took until Tennessee to get her to stop crying. Getting a chameleon off one's lip isn't as easy as it sounds, and if it ever happens to you, here's Ellen's piece of advice for the year. Avoid pulling the chameleon by the tail or straight off the lip. That only makes it clutch on harder. Instead, apply slight pressure to the base of the neck (the chameleon's neck, not the crying child's, as much as you'd like to at that moment), and the instant that little sucker opens its mouth, remove immediately. You'll thank Ellen for that piece of advice one day. Well, now it's December and Christmas is upon us. And all Kevin and Ellen want is just five minutes of peace and quiet. Beth wants a basketball. Kelly wants a chameleon. Julie doesn't.

Merry Christmas from Kevin, Ellen, Beth, Julie, and Kelly Sutton.

1994

Attention, K-Mart shoppers.

The year 1994 is almost over. And the entire year can be encapsulated in one incident in January. Ellen sent Kevin to K-Mart to find a pair of plain white canvas shoes for Beth. No problem, right? Ah, but this was K-Mart. ("Have you ever been turned down for a government job because you were just too damn incompetent?" *"Uh, what government?"* "Good answer, you're K-Mart management material.") When Beth and Kevin got there, they found that an entire section of shoes, from size eleven to size two, was missing. (Beth wore size one.) Obviously, something was amiss. After ten minutes of searching, Kevin reluctantly decided to seek help from the K-Mart staff. (Hint: the *K* does not stand for *knowledgeable*.) Big mistake. Kevin asked the first employee who walked by if he could help them find some shoes. "That ain't my department. I'll send someone back." Seven minutes later, nobody came back. All that time employees would enter and come out of the swinging doors leading back to whatever it is behind those swinging doors (one thing is for certain, it's not an Ivy League recruitment office), and every attempt at getting help ended up the same. "That ain't my department." Twenty minutes later, his patience thinner than the plot of a Sylvester Stallone movie, Kevin went on a mission. Find the competent K-Mart employee. Which, it turns out, is considerably harder than finding Waldo. One lady, while she didn't work in that department, did agree to page someone to

"Shoes" (K-Mart's secret code for "The Shoe Department"—you may need that information someday). After ten minutes, nobody came back. Peeved, Kevin decided it was time to take matters into his own hands. Literally. He went to the K-Mart phone, hit "page" and began, over the entire store intercom, what started out as a simple expletive-laced assessment of K-Mart that turned into an expletive-laced indictment of the entire service industry, followed by an expletive-laced request for help in "Shoes." Still, nobody came back. When Kevin and Beth returned home empty-footed, Ellen asked Beth where her shoes were. She replied, "They didn't have any, Mommy. But Daddy was on the radio at K-Mart." In February, Beth eventually found shoes and joined a new basketball team. She even scored a few times. (Speaking of scoring, in February Kevin and Ellen found out they were going to have yet another child.) Beth was the defensive star of the team. One game she stole the ball from the best girl on the other team three times. Later, when Ellen asked her how she did it, she replied, "I just got in her face and yelled, 'Give me the ball, give me the ball, give me the ball,' and it scared her and she gave me the ball." The next day Kevin went into his boss's office, got in his face and yelled, "Give me a raise, give me a raise, give me a raise," and it scared him and he didn't give Kevin a raise. Life, it seems, does not imitate sports. In March, Kevin left his job in Birmingham and moved to Dallas. A few months later, Ellen discovered he had moved, tracked him down after an exhaustive search, and in June moved the family to Dallas. For the record, when you move from Alabama, you are no longer required by law to leave with a banjo, or any other musical or medical instrument, on your knee. In March, Julie and Kelly turned five. It finally dawned on Kevin and Ellen that the term Terrible Twos did not refer to age, but to the two of them. They started T-ball in April. Started making excuses for not paying attention in T-ball in May. And started to actually be an asset to their T-ball team in June. Which was when they moved to Dallas. Speaking of which, the move was a nightmare. (Hint: K-Mart would be well-served to hire Allied Van Lines people.) You could say Allied dropped the ball on the move, but that wouldn't be giving them their due credit. They dropped not just the ball, but everything. Ellen dropped the kid in August. August 3. Caroline Lucille (named after her great-grandmother) checked in during *Letterman*. Good thing it was a rerun. Julie suddenly had a purpose in life. "I will give her smiling lessons." Let's just hope she doesn't give Caroline crying lessons. If she does, then at least Caroline will be learning at the feet of the master. Julie and Kelly started kindergarten in August. On the first day, Ellen and Kevin sent apology notes to their teachers in advance. Somehow, though, Julie won the Citizen of the Week award at school. Kevin and Ellen were so proud. Maybe Julie could be good after all. Then they found out it was a random selection. And life as they knew it made sense once again. It's December now and the twins' first year of school is nearly half over. Beth is doing well in third grade and in basketball. Caroline is such a good baby, Kevin and Ellen wish they had more like her. (Scratch that last thought.) And to top it off, Kevin's new agency is trying to get K-Mart's advertising account. In the presentation he informed them he already has extensive experience working on K-Mart radio announcements. That should give him a leg up. In the meantime, one thought gives Kevin and Ellen hope to continue on each day. Only eighteen more years until all the kids are out of the house.

Merry Christmas and Happy New Year from Kevin, Ellen, Beth, Julie, and Kelly. And introducing Caroline Sutton.

BABIES ARE DUMB

If babies were smart, they could negotiate a thousand-dollar-a-week allowance from their parents the minute they're born. If only they had the cognitive skills to form words:

"Look, Dad, I know you hate having to extract the hunk of crap that's in my diaper six times a day as well as sop up the thirty pounds of pee I generate hourly, so here's what I'm going to do. What's it worth to you if I learn that toilet thing right now, today? Fifty bucks? You're kidding, right? Do I look like I was born yesterday? OK, I was. But do I look that way? I do? Well, fifty bucks isn't going to cut it. My price? I was thinking more like a grand. Ha, a grand a year? How quaint. No, I mean a grand a week. You think I'm being immature? Hell, Dad, I'm just thirty-five hours old. Besides, who peed in the boss's fern tree at the company Christmas party last year? Yeah, I heard about that. OK, if you're not willing to go to a grand a week, that's fine— Oh, hang on. I feel a big one coming. It's big and it's tarlike and it's really going to be hard to scrape off. You don't mind scraping my tarlike stools off my legs, do you? Oh, and be careful, because my urinator could go off at any moment. Oops, there it is. Sorry, Old

Man. My bad. So, you want to talk about that thousand dollars a week now, huh? What? You want to compromise? OK, how about, uh, a thousand dollars a week? What do you mean, I didn't compromise? I *am* promising to use that toilet thing. I don't have to do that, you know? I could go another two and a half years. Yes, two and a half years is about average. I know a thousand dollars a week is a bit steep. But— Uh-oh, here comes Mount Saint Helens again. Don't you just *lava* that smell? Oh, and all over your new shirt. Funny how shirt and shit are almost spelled the same, isn't it? Well, excuse me, but I find that funny. So, back to that thousand bucks a wee-wee-wee— Oh, there it goes again, like Old Faithful. Quit pleading. You are embarrassing yourself. What? You've upped your offer? Really, I don't need a thousand dollars a day. That's quite generous, really. How about you give me a thousand dollars a week like I asked in the first place and I will learn that toilet thing right now? I mean, how hard can it be? You learned it. OK, thanks, Dad. Money well spent. I am going back to being your cute little baby again. Ha, that was a funny joke, Dad. Pissing away money. I get it. Good one, Old Man."

If babies weren't stupid, they'd be rich.

THE MOST PERFECT PARENTS ON EARTH

When you have your first child, you decide that every other parent who came before you was awful at it and you are going to be the best parents ever. You have it figured out. You've read articles on it. You've read books. Many of those written by childless loners who live with cats.

Ellen and I were the same way. Beth was our little girl and she was going to be the most precious, most special, most cared-for girl in the history of babyhood. The perfect parents were going to raise the perfect child.

We were perfect dumbasses.

Before we gave her a bottle, we'd boil the organic German Nano-latex antibacterial nipples in a solution of 100 percent pure Icelandic mountain stream water and unicorn tears.

Her clothes were hand washed with a toxin-free, fragrance-free, natural organic saponified laundry detergent in a resin-free basin filled with a mixture of distilled polar icecap drippings and unicorn tears.

When she'd drop her pacifier on the floor, we quickly purified it in a boiling solution of natural spring water imported from an underground Parisian aquifer, then cooled it gently in a jar of Swiss mountain air, then spritzed it with a mild solution of coconut water and unicorn tears before delicately reinserting it into her vomit hole.

By the time our fifth daughter, Katie, came around, we'd wipe off the nipples under our armpits, and if she dropped her pacifier, we'd have the dog lick off any germs, and then shove it back into her suck hole.

They both seem to have turned out OK.

MY BABY WROTE ME A LETTER

The classic 1960s song "The Letter" by the Box Tops was playing in the delivery room the very moment my wife Ellen went into labor with our first daughter, the very moment the neonatal nurses at St. Vincent Hospital in Indianapolis went into baby delivering mode, and the very moment my financial future went into past tense.

I remember thinking about the irony of the lyrics. It was as if the song was literally speaking to me, "Hey, pal, hop on the next aeroplane and get your ass out of Dodge."

It was a warning. And like most warnings, especially the one about not reusing condoms, I did not heed it.

My ass stayed in Dodge.

I stayed because a few minutes later, after my wife made the grunting noises that accompany what women call labor—which really in no way resembles interstate trucking or welding rivets or any activity concerning any labor union in America because there is no paycheck for it and thus no chance to collect union dues— out popped something that forever changed my life.

My first daughter. Elizabeth.

I have to say, it was an incredible moment. It reminded me of the other incredible moment in my life just three years prior in Cincinnati, when the Reds were honoring their legendary catcher Johnny Bench who was playing his last game. Magically, as if on cue, he hit a game-tying home run into a sign that read, of all things: "HIT YOUR LAST ONE HERE, JOHNNY." Fifty thousand fans cheered the loudest, most joyous collective noise I had ever heard. Grown men cried in Riverfront Stadium. I cried in Riverfront Stadium. Just as I cried in the delivery room at St. Vincent Hospital.

Watching Beth being born was right up there with Johnny Bench Night. Only they didn't serve beer.

It was the single best moment in my life. OK, so maybe it wasn't so good six months later when she had just been fed and I was playing with her by holding her in the air Superman-style while I laughed and laughed and laughed, and while she laughed and laughed and vomited. Directly into my mouth.

But vomiting in my mouth was still six months into the future. At that moment her round blue eyes looked directly at me and she smiled. Yes, she smiled. I am telling you, she smiled.

"Oh, that's just gas," the nurse told me, mocking me in a tone designed to make me look stupid.

"Gas?" I shot back at her. "What? Did she grab a quick burrito and a soda on the way out?"

My new daughter smiled at me. The least I could do was to smile back.

For the first time, my life had a purpose, to be the sun in this planet's solar system.

I was Beth's dad.

I sat down and held her and just stared. I looked at her sweet round face, her soft thin hair, her little fingers, her candy corn toes. Then, for some reason, a wave of practicality swept over me. And I started thinking about things like diapers and clothes and food and braces and cars and college tuition and a wedding.

I recalled a statistic that said the average cost of raising a daughter is nearly four hundred fifty thousand dollars.

Reality set in. *I am so screwed.*

It was too late to send her back. St. Vincent had a strict no-return policy.

The last line of the song's lyrics played: *My baby, she wrote me a letter.*

I read that letter. It said, "You pay now."

IT'S A GIRL, IT'S ANOTHER GIRL

If you are so "blessed" to learn that your wife is going to give birth to twins, one word of warning: your wife is going to turn mean. I mean, *mean*.

Mine was so nasty to the car salesman showing us a new minivan that I felt compelled to buy it right there on the spot. No joke. I felt sorry for the guy. I even tossed in free undercoating on his car. Apparently the guy didn't walk fast enough through the lot for someone (hint: that someone wasn't me).

You will discover a level of snippiness that goes well past an eleven on the dial. Good luck.

In her defense, perhaps one reason she had become a card-carrying member of Our Sisters of Perpetual Agitation was because every day toward the end of her pregnancy, every single person we knew would call and say, "Have you had the twins yet?"

This was before Facebook, when if you wanted to communicate with people you had to go through the distasteful act of actually communicating with them. So it got a little old fielding calls about the twins when all she wanted was to have them ripped from her body that very second.

Even my own mother would call every day. So one time I told her, "Oh, shoot, Mom, I forgot to tell you, we had them six days ago. Sorry, but you can imagine how busy I've been."

I heard that long, familiar, you've-disappointed-your-mother-again sigh I grew up with. She let out a thin, "You did?"

"Come on, Mom, I was just joking. Don't you think you'd be the first person on the planet that I'd call when they pop out?"

Well, as twins often do, ours popped out weeks early. That day the hospital was a madhouse. Having twins is considered a high-risk pregnancy. For the hospital, it's winning the lottery. In the delivery room are: 1) Three doctors—one for each kid, one for the mom, zero for the dad. 2) Three nurses—one for each kid, one for the mom, zero for the dad. 3) An anesthesiologist with an assistant who, by the way, offers no assistance to the dad. 4) A sonogram assistant, see preceding description of assistant. 5) Two birth attendants who, like restroom attendants in classy restaurants, appear to work for tips.

Julie came out first. Kelly was supposed to slide out right after that. But the twins had a preliminary bout before all the main events they would share with us over the next eighteen years. It seems Julie got in one last free kick on Kelly, and a free farewell hair pull, which spun Kelly upside down. So they had to do a Scissorian. They told me I had to leave. Not one of the assistants assisted me out.

Fifteen minutes later, Kelly was born. Six days later, I called my mom to tell her the happy news.

Suddenly we went from one daughter to three, all under the age of three. From man-to-man to zone.

Having twins is natural birth control. You never, ever again want to do anything close to what you did that made that happen.

Mathematically, having twins means twice the diapers, twice the feedings, twice the making a deal with the devil to get them to sleep. But in reality, it's like having a baby that eats and craps 24/7, and sleeps 0/7. One twin or the other is always getting fed or changed, and when you finally get that one down, the other one pops up for its turn. Not even the finest minds at the Jack Daniels Company of Lynchburg, Tennessee, have come up with a cure for twins.

Ellen was a milking machine for the first year of the twins' lives.

It didn't help that they were born with sleep apnea. They would randomly stop breathing in their sleep. For the first nine months of their lives, we had to strap a breathing monitor onto each of them, day and night, in case they fell asleep. When one stopped breathing, a piercing alarm would sound and we'd have to race into their room to wake that one by startling her into breathing. The alarm usually woke the other one, crying. Most nights I slept on the floor between their cribs. I discovered it was actually quieter than the constant hum of the milking machines in the dairy production barn called our bedroom.

Again I say, natural birth control.

But before we got to take them home, they had to stay in the hospital, in incubators, for about ten days in order to let their lungs develop the strength to breathe on their own. Ellen stayed with them most of the day. I would come after work and at lunch.

One evening after work, I came to the hospital to find Ellen crying hysterically and Kelly not in her incubator.

"What's wrong?" I asked.

Ellen tried to speak, but was so shaken she could barely form words: "Sh-sh-she died."

No words can describe my devastation at that point. Now I was the one who couldn't breathe. I didn't want to breathe. I was numb. The world ended.

Then the nurse came in holding a baby with green nail polish on its left big toe. We had painted Kelly's green and Julie's red so we could tell them apart.

It was Kelly. My mind tried to figure out what was happening. Did she mean Julie? No, Julie was there, and she was fine.

"Ellen, what did you say to me?"

She was a bit calmer now that Kelly was with us. "Sh-she did it." She had tried to tell me that Kelly had set off her monitor again.

Somebody should develop an app that can translate Female into Male. The roller coaster of emotions I went through in that thirty seconds was something I never want to experience again. I held Kelly for hours.

Sixteen years after that night, Kelly asked for a car for her birthday. I couldn't say no.

Well played, Kelly.

SHITTING MACHINES

"Daddy, Daddy, Daddy!"

It's always amazed me the sheer tonnage of stuff that can come out of a little girl. It defies physics.

One night when Beth was three, right after she finally got out of her crib and into a bed, she got out of that bed and walked into our room.

"Daddy, Daddy, Daddy!"

She had the sense not to go to Ellen's side of the bed, where her request would be met with the same level of success with which I am met when I venture to that side of the bed at night.

So Beth walked over to my side of the bed and began trying to wake me.

"Daddy, Daddy, Daddy!"

At first I wasn't sure if what I was hearing was my daughter's sweet voice, or if I had simply left the TV on Cinemax's encore showing of *Naughty Nurses Eleven* (which, despite what the critics say, is a shallow follow-up to *NN Ten*).

I opened one eye. The TV was off. So I looked to my right. My sweet little girl was standing next to me.

"Daddy, Daddy, Daddy!"

"What? What's happening?"

"Something came out of me."

"Huh?"

"Something came out of me."

Before I could wrap my brain around what she was trying to tell me, my cute-as-a-button little girl in her Little Mermaid nightgown and Cookie Monster slippers vomited all over me.

Hot bubbling vomit.

While Ellen slept soundly, and trying not to gag, I followed a trail of vomit from my face, out of our bedroom, down the hallway, over the cat (which made me chuckle), into Beth's room, and all over her new bed and sheets.

While Ellen slept soundly, I made a rough calculation that about eighty-two pounds of vomit came out of a thirty-one-pound girl. Nearly three times her body weight.

But when you have kids you realize how that is possible. Because that little kid was, at one time, a tiny baby. And from the time they are born, babies are basically just shitting machines.

Until a baby is old enough to do anything on his or her own, like crawl or sit up or order online with your American Express card, they pretty much just eat and shit.

In goes food, out comes shit. In goes food, out comes shit. In goes food, out comes shit. Like the revolving door of NFL players being booked into custody, it never ends.

I've often heard experienced parents trying to ease the minds of first-time expecting couples with, "Oh, it doesn't smell that bad at first, not until they start eating real food."

That's a crock of shit. Shit smells like shit. That's why it's called shit.

Face it, that adorable little thing you bring home from the hospital is a shitting machine in disguise.

Do you immediately run out and buy the thing a baseball glove or a computer or drums or a backyard Jarts set? No. The first thing you buy is diapers.

And the second thing. And the fifth thing. And the one-hundred-thousand-seven-hundred-ninety-second thing.

Because you soon learn the problem with this new shitting machine you've just brought home is that, unless you're a dung beetle, Pitbull's producer, or a show runner for reality TV, nobody likes being surrounded by crap.

So you buy diapers. And more diapers. And more diapers. Which explains why diaper sales in America are roughly 5.4 billion dollars a year.

It brings new meaning to the term disposable income. Nearly every penny you make in the first two years of that baby's life will be spent on diapers.

For our first girl we did cloth diapers. What a weird ordeal that is. To begin with, it requires that you store a nuclear dump in your house—a big bin of used, dirty diapers. Imagine a toilet you don't flush. Imagine Fresno.

Diaper changing becomes a game. How quickly can you remove that crap-soaked diaper, open the lid to the nuclear storage bin where you are exposed to the deadly toxic aroma of days-old crap-soaked diapers, and get the lid closed again before you faint?

My record was 1.6 seconds.

If that's not weird enough, think about what happens next. Once a week you wrap up that bag of smelly, crap-infused diapers and put it on your porch, where some guy comes by and takes it to headquarters, where some other guy has to—I don't even want to think about what that guy has to do. Scrape the diapers? Scrub off the crap? Other than Madonna's gynecologist, I cannot imagine a nastier job in America than cleaning the crap off used cloth diapers.

Once we had twins, we went with disposable diapers because life got way too hectic to keep up with cloth.

Now of course, a lot of people who have never had children will try making you feel guilty for buying disposable diapers.

"Think about what it's doing to the landfills," they whine. "Think of the landfills."

Come to think of it, roughly a quarter of what's in there came from my house. Thank you, Mr. Landfill.

An interesting fact, though, and one that doomsday environmentalists don't want you to know, is that landfill space in America is shrinking dramatically. In 1986, when I had my first daughter, there were nearly eight thousand landfills in the United States. Today, there are around eleven hundred.

Is it because Americans are so good with recycling? Partially.

Is it because technology has increased to a point that landfill companies can squeeze twice the amount of trash into the same space they could before? Partially.

But the real reason can be summed up in one word.

China.

Despite the incredible trade imbalance we have with China in nearly every economic category, and despite the fact that China is just about a quarter of an inch away from buying the United States in a garage sale, there is one major export category America dominates with China.

Trash.

China is the leading importer of trash from the United States. Ironic, when you think about it, since everything made in China is crap. They buy it from us, mark it up, and sell it back to us for a profit.

China is a big country. Bigger than ten Oprahs. We won't be running out of landfill space on this Earth for thousands of generations.

Don't let anyone guilt you into avoiding disposable diapers if that's what you want to do.

There will always be China.

1995

Elvis is still dead,
Ellen is still pregnant.

How did 1995 go for the Suttons? We'll tell you how 1995 went for the Suttons. On August 16, at 8:47 p.m., Kevin was minding his own business, washing the dishes. The kids were asleep. All four of them. Four. He thought Ellen was upstairs working. Instead, she was taking a test. She came downstairs and showed Kevin the results of that test. "Hey, look at this," she said. Kevin turned around, saw what she was holding, dropped a dish, and stared. It was one of those "oh my God, don't tell me that's a home pregnancy test you're holding in your hand and it's positive and you're pregnant again and we're going to have five kids and we're not even Catholic or on welfare" stares. You know the look. When the absolutely unheard of is suddenly heard of. You had it on your face the day you saw Lisa Marie go on TV and say that she and Michael really do it. Five kids. Five little bundles of joy. Like Julie, for instance. In March, Kevin took her to Toys"R"Us to buy a birthday present for her twin sister, Kelly. It went something like this: "I want that for myself." *"No."* "I want that for myself." *"No."* "I want that for myself." *"No."* "I want that for myself." *"No."* "I want that for myself." *"No."* "I want that for myself." *"No."* Finally, he'd had enough. Kevin grabbed her by the arm and said (follow along, it's from page 287 in the Parent Handbook), "Look, (name of child), you've got to realize you can't always get everything you want. That's just the way life works." At that moment Julie decided to change the vote on her Dad of the Year ballot. Well, about thirty minutes went by without Julie saying a single word to Kevin. As they were in the car heading home, Julie reached into her pocket and pulled out a roll of Life Savers. "Hey, Daddy, do you want a Life Saver?" Kevin's heart melted. His little Julie was growing up. She was making that leap from infantile kid to forgiving little girl. Kevin almost wept. "Sure, Julie, I'd love one," Kevin replied proudly to his newly maturing daughter. "Too bad, Daddy. You've got to realize you can't always get everything you want. That's just the way life works," she said. Then she popped a Life Saver into her mouth, shoved the roll back into her pocket, and coldly turned away. It was then, right there and then, that the light switch in his head clicked into the "on" position and everything suddenly became clear: he was raising females. Like Kelly. Over the Fourth of July holiday, Kevin and Ellen loaded up the Screaming Baby Express and pointed it north. The road from Dallas to Indianapolis runs through Memphis. That's where Elvis's house is. Right there between a strip joint and a Jiffy Lube (which are really one and the same, if you think about it). "How many times do you pass through Memphis?" Kevin and Ellen wondered. (They're not looking for an exact count here, so put away your calculator.) "Let's stop at Graceland, show the kids a piece of history, get in a few good laughs, see what kind of carpeting K-Mart was selling in the sixties," Kevin announced to his family. Kelly had no idea who Elvis was and, being Kelly, she asked questions. Lots of questions: "Who is Elvis?" *"He was big in the fifties. Then got even bigger in the seventies."* "Is Elvis still alive?" *"Depends on which papers you read."* "How did he die?" *"He took drugs."* (Here was a good time to work in an antidrug message.) *"You know, Kelly, drugs are the second-leading cause of death among young people. Right behind O. J. Simpson."* Well, the trip to Graceland was everything they expected. The safari room with the jungle motif. The TV room with the bright yellow-and-blue carpeting and the lightning bolt on the wall. The game room that felt like being trapped in a purple velour cave. Much to the chagrin of the tour guides, in every room Kelly would shout out inquisitively, and at a decibel level higher than Elvis ever got on goofballs, "DID ELVIS EAT DRUGS IN THIS ROOM, MOMMY? DID ELVIS EAT DRUGS IN THIS ROOM?" Chances are pretty good that the Suttons will not be receiving a Christmas card from

Graceland this year. By the way, the world has been horribly misinformed about how Elvis died. Not from a drug overdose, as the liberal media would have us believe. It was from "an overreliance on medication," as the tour guides so kindly pointed out. After visiting Graceland, however, Kevin is convinced Elvis simply died of retina damage. Speaking of eye trouble, Beth got glasses this year. Now she can read signs along the road really well. Kevin uses that to his advantage. One particularly typical day while the kids were being shuttled around, they decided they'd play a friendly game of Let's Pull Out Each Other's Hair. Beth said she didn't see what happened. Which meant Beth started it. The Screaming Baby Express was in full force once again. There was shrieking and yelling and crying and girl slapping. It was getting ugly. Hillary ugly (whether you lean to the left or lean to the right, you have to admit you'd lean a tad away if you were standing next to her). Kevin was just about ready to (from page 196 of the Handbook) pull the car over and come back there and do whatever it is parents do when they threaten to come back there. In fact, he'd gotten the first few words out. "If you girls don't knock it off I'm going to—" when suddenly, up ahead, he saw a man standing on the side of the road holding a sign. Not one to let a golden opportunity pass, Kevin acted fast. "Hey, Beth, let's see how well your new glasses work. See if you can read that sign." She let go of the clump of Julie's hair and read it out loud: "Children...Killed...Here." (Apparently he was some sort of abortion protester standing outside a clinic.) The kids' eyes got wide with horror. "If you girls don't knock it off I'm going to...I'm going to drop you off at this store right now." The remainder of the car ride was, for some reason, perfectly quiet. Page forty-seven: Fear, the Great Silencer. Well, anyway, in a nutshell, that's what 1995 was like for the Suttons. Ellen is due in February. (Another girl, as if you needed to be told.) Kevin is having a TV set and a urinal installed in his walk-in closet so he can have someplace he can just go and live his life in peace. Beth is in fourth grade, Julie and Kelly are in first grade. And Caroline is sixteen months old, has turned into the happiest, friendliest little baby, and goes to Mother's Day Out (Ellen is the patron saint of the place) every Wednesday. All, as you can tell, is fine in Dallas. We hope all is fine with you as well. Happy New Year. And if you don't get everything you want for Christmas, well, too bad. You've got to realize you can't always get everything you want. That's just the way life works.

Merry Christmas from Kevin, Ellen, Beth, Julie, Kelly, and Caroline Sutton.

1996

You hate me and I have proof.

The Suttons started 1996 with four children. They're ending it with five. As you can see, the Suttons are overstocked. So they're having their year-end inventory reduction sale. Come on down and make a deal. No reasonable offer will be refused. Trade-ins accepted. You buy here, you pay here. Financing is available on the spot. Yes, once again, this was an interesting year at the Suttons. It all began in January (as most years do), when Ellen asked Kevin, "What's wrong with Julie?" *"You mean, right now? Or always?"* Julie had been sulking around for days, in one of those particularly female moods. You know the kind. Where the littlest of things make them fly off the biggest of handles. Anyway, after three days of this, Kevin had finally had enough. *"Julie, what's bugging you?"* "Nothing." *"I know something is wrong. What is it?"* "Nothing." *"Come on, Julie, you can tell me."* "Nothing." *"All right, then I guess nothing's bothering you."* Kevin started to walk away when Julie shot back, "Well, if you don't know, I'm not going to tell you." (A deep sense of satisfaction crept across Ellen's heart. Her little girl was turning into a woman.) "You hate me, Daddy," Julie finally blurted out. *"No, I don't."* "Yes, you do." *"No, I don't."* "Yes, you do." *"No, I don't."* "Yes, you do." *"No, I don't."* "Yes, you do." (Note to Julie's future husband: Run now. Run like hell. Run far and never turn back.) "You hate me and I have proof." *"What are you talking about?"* "I asked the Magic Eight Ball if you hate me and it said yes, and

Beth told me the Magic Eight Ball is true and that means you hate me, and I am going to run away." Kevin hates the Magic Eight Ball. In a related Ball of Magic story, also in January, Kevin had the surgery to make sure there would be no more Julies. After much consternation, and considerable swelling, they are happy to report everything went well. Ellen has, however, noticed a few slight changes in Kevin. For one, he just likes to cuddle now. He also gets really, really miffed when people badmouth Martha Stewart. And every once in a while, on a whim, he'll hop in the car and go to Cloth World, you know, just to browse. Other than that, though, everything is fine. Child Five came in February. Ellen is such a pro at it now, she had the baby in between loads of laundry. Needless to say, it was another girl. Ellen and Kevin named her Caroline. No, wait, that was Child Four. This one they named, uh, oh yeah, Katharine. Katharine Michelle. Born Valentine's Day 1996. They call her Katie. Caroline calls her WrestleMania partner. In March, Julie slugged Kelly. Kelly cried. Kelly kicked Julie. Julie cried. In April, Julie slugged Kelly. Kelly cried. Kelly kicked Julie. Julie cried. (If this is starting to get old to you, it's getting real old to Kevin and Ellen, too.) Besides the beatings and near-death strangulations, there were other developments. After seven long and proud years of service, Kevin and Ellen finally put the Screaming Baby Express out to pasture. They traded in the old, drab minivan for a new, drab minivan. Screaming Baby Express Two. Coming to a town near you. Look for it. (And when you see it, run. Run like hell. Run far and never look back.) Beth is in fifth grade. She's cheerleading now. Which makes Ellen nervous, seeing as how Texas is the state where moms pay hit men to knock off other cheerleaders' moms. She's keeping her eyes open. The twins are in second grade. Julie plays the guitar. Kelly plays piano. ("I play piano better than you play guitar." "No, you don't." "Yes, I do.") They recently started a nightly feature right after their shower called Naked Girl Boxing. So far, Julie is up fifteen bouts to twelve, with three draws and two I'm-Telling-Mommy-You-Kicked-Mes. Apparently, kicking is a violation of International Naked Girl Boxing Federation regulations. Caroline is beginning her initiation into the local street gang by scribbling graffiti on every flat surface in the house. And Katie is ten months old and just now starting to utter her first words. (They were, "Mommy, can I go back in for a while?") So there you have it. Another year gone by in Dallas. And every day when Kevin comes home from work he looks around at this household of his, at his family with their cherry-red cheeks and glowing smiles, all nestled around the dinner table. Five daughters. One wife. Six females. And, every day, as he reflects on the fruits that have been bestowed upon him, Kevin looks up to the heavens and says to God, "You hate me and I have proof."

Merry Christmas from Kevin, Ellen, Beth, Julie, Kelly, Caroline, and the new one, Katharine Sutton. (We can't even say Merry Christmas without taking up two lines now.)

1997

Questions, questions, questions.

As the last few days of 1997 trickle away, it's time for Kevin and Ellen to reflect on the fruits that have been bestowed upon them over the past twelve months. (OK, so maybe the fruit was more like soggy bruised bananas than, say, crisp, ripe golden apples.) It was our first full year with five daughters. Unlike that couple in Iowa who took the easy way out and had a litter of kids all at one time, ours was done the excruciatingly slow way, over the course of ten years and without the use of chemicals—well, if you don't count that wine that makes Ellen so "friendly." People seemed to have this strange fascination with our having five daughters. No matter where we went this year, people asked us the same questions over and over. (Not counting, "Will you please never come back again?" which is a whole different discussion altogether.) For instance, they'd ask, "What's it feel like to have five daughters?" That's a tough question to answer. After all, some things are just impossible to describe. Like, how do you tell someone what it feels like when you snag a hangnail and it rips out from that tender part of your finger and constantly throbs in red-hot agony? Or how can you describe the feeling you get when a tiny little sliver of glass gets stuck in the ball of your foot and then every time you take a step and put some weight on it, it sends a sharp, shooting, localized pain throughout your body? You just can't describe a thing like that. But perhaps the following anecdote will help. On October 14, 1997, at precisely 6:21

Central Standard Time, Phase Four of Ellen's diabolical plan to indoctrinate all five offspring into the sisterhood of Sisterhood was complete. Caroline—little, innocent, sweet, three-year-old Caroline—was whining. Kevin noticed, however, it wasn't her usual little, innocent, sweet, three-year-old's whine. No, this whine had a purpose. An intensity. A femaleness. Kevin looked at his pitiful, crying daughter. Her bottom lip was sticking out and quivering and there was actual tearing. Something was different. "What's wrong, Caroline?" Kevin asked. And then, at that very moment, the one thing Kevin had been dreading since the day Caroline was born happened. She said, "I don't have everything, Daddy. And I want *everything*." And at that very moment, Caroline officially went from female to Female. (The certification papers arrived from headquarters the next day, via FedEx. They're very efficient, you know.) Ellen smiled. Four down, one to go. Beth, Julie, Kelly, and now Caroline. Her work on this planet was almost complete. Only Katie was left. Little, innocent, sweet, twenty-month-old Katie. Her apprenticeship is off to a good start, however. When she doesn't want something, she doesn't just say no, like a typical baby. She says, "No way," like an Ellen baby. See if you can spot a similarity: Exhibit A) *"It's time for your nap now, Katie."* "No way." Exhibit B) *"Hey, Ellen, I was thinking about playing poker with—"* "No way." The defense rests. Another question people always ask us is, "Do you have any idea how much five weddings are going to cost you?" We do have some idea. But, just in case, Kevin has a backup plan. Every Wednesday night at eight thirty, he gathers the girls in the family room, makes up a big batch of popcorn, turns on the television and says, "Girls, this program is called *Ellen*. It stars a lady named Ellen DeGeneres. Just, well, just watch it." Hey, sometimes a father of five girls has got to do what a father of five girls has got to do. He's not sure if it's having any effect. But he has noticed WNBA scouts checking out Beth and Julie and Kelly lately. The question which always follows that one is, "Do you have any idea how much college is going to cost?" College? They're girls. They don't have to be smart, just pretty. Besides, how expensive can the Dallas College of Cosmetology really be, anyway? Another question people asked us a million times this year: "Five daughters. Were you trying for a boy?" A few months ago, in a restaurant, Beth answered that with perhaps the best response of all. "See those four girls?" she said, pointing to her sisters. "Those were the tries." So that's pretty much how 1997 went in the Sutton family. Endless questions. Can I have candy? Can I get contacts? Will that patch of hair Kelly just pulled from Julie's scalp grow back? Can I have my ears pierced? Are all boys stupid? Do you have Lorena Bobbitt's phone number? Beth's in sixth grade. She recently won the free-throw championship for her school and will go up against champs from other schools. Julie and Kelly are in third grade. Julie led her softball team in home runs and grand slams. Kelly led her basketball team in points scored and hissy fits. Caroline is three and, just like what happened to Kelly when she was three, she got hit in the head with a baseball bat this summer while playing in the front yard. Which means 40 percent of our children have now been hit in the head with baseball bats, much higher than the national average. It makes Kevin and Ellen all tingly inside knowing their kids are better than average. Katie is closing in on two and trying hard to figure out what she did to deserve all this. All of which leads to the one other question Kevin and Ellen heard over and over and over again this year: "Five daughters. So are you going to have another one?" People can be so cruel.

Merry Christmas and Happy New Year from Kevin, Ellen, Beth, Julie, Kelly, Caroline, and Katie Sutton. Any questions?

I HATE YOU

The first time your daughter tells you she hates you, it crushes you inside. I mean, you're the guy who did that airplane thingy over and over and over again while mean Mommy yelled, "Put her down, you're going to drop her." You're the guy who gave her Girl Scout cookies for breakfast before mean Mommy came downstairs and got all over you for ruining her health with cookies for breakfast as she poured her a proper breakfast of Cocoa Puffs. You're the guy who let her wear the pink ballerina dress with that green shirt and those red cowboy boots to school when mean Mommy picked out that stupid itchy polka-dot dress.

You thought you were buddies, pals for life. Then she tells you she hates you. It's devastating.

Get over it.

After about the tenth time you hear that, it occurs to you, oh yeah, a little girl is just a not-quite-yet-formed woman. Her irrationality, lack of accountability, and lack of concern for hurting one's feelings haven't been honed to soul-crushing perfection. Yet.

So ignore it.

I have gotten dozens of "I hate you" notes from my daughters. They always thoughtfully included a drawing of a horse or a puppy or a little girl crying. One particular note from Caroline read: "Dear Dad, I hate you from the bottom of my heart, which is something you don't have." She was kind enough to sign it, "Sincerely, Caroline." I appreciated the sincerity, and the drawing of a heart. Since I didn't have one, it was nice to know what one looked like. Someday I can take that into my cardiologist and say, "If you find one of these, fix it."

One day my little sweet Katie, my *Simpsons*-watching buddy, my ice cream store accomplice, told me she hated me because I wouldn't let her go to an indoor rock-climbing party, since two days before she was put into a cast for a broken elbow and trying to climb a rock wall with that broken elbow was exactly the sort of thing her doctor told her not to do.

"I hate you, Daddy."

So I asked her, "Wait a second, how can you hate me? You don't even really know me that well. You only just met me the day you were born, and that wasn't really even your choice. You don't know my favorite whiskey, or who I voted for in the last election, or which charities I contribute to. You don't know if I cheat on my taxes, or what my favorite song from the band America is, or whether I am a habitual tailgater, or what my stance on abortion is. (It tends to fluctuate after they tell you they hate you.) You don't really know me well enough to hate me yet. Give it some time."

That was eight years ago. Plenty of time.

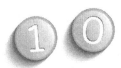

CAN AND WILL BE USED AGAINST YOU

Kids have an unbelievable capacity to remember things. It occurred to me one day why that is. They have nothing else in their little brains getting in the way.

They aren't going, "You think the banking industry will make another greedy money grab and cause the subprime market to tank, triggering widespread panic that will wipe out our college tuitions and force Dad into sleepless nights, worried about how he is going to provide for his family?"

No, basically it's, "Poop, cookie, lollipop, toy, more poop, cookie, lollipop, ice cream, more poop."

Once, when I was coaching my six-year-old twins in softball and they weren't paying attention, I started wondering why. I mean, what could they possibly be thinking about out there? Julie was just kind of drifting off, wandering around in a fog. So when she came back to the bench, curiosity got the better of me.

"Julie," I asked, "when you're out there playing, what are you thinking about?"

"Pooping."

I've often wondered if Nelson Cruz failed to catch that ball in game six that cost the Texas Rangers the 2011 World Series championship because he was thinking of taking a dump.

We moved to Birmingham from Indianapolis, when Beth was four and the twins were one, in the summer of 1990. Our backyard had an empty field behind it with a ton of trees. So when fall came I discovered the joy of raking, along with the joy of raking with kids, who never see a pile they can't destroy by jumping in. Since kids don't get paid, they don't understand the concept of having to do work over again.

We were all out raking leaves when Beth looked up at me and said, "I love you, Daddy. I want to marry you."

"That's sweet, Beth, but you're my daughter; we can't get married. We don't live in Kentucky."

On many occasions, Ellen fails to share my sense of humor. That was one such occasion. "You shouldn't tell Beth things like that," she said.

"Oh, it's just a joke, don't worry."

Three months later we decided to make that first drive back north for the holidays.

When we're on a long car trip, Ellen likes informing the girls where we are. "Look, kids, we're in Tennessee."

A couple of hours later, "We're in Kentucky."

Without missing a beat, Beth piped up, "We can get married now, Daddy!"

I thought, *Holy shit, she remembered that? That was months ago.*

Ellen looked at me with that look where boners go to die and said, "You're an idiot."

Moral of the story: don't ever say anything to your kids.

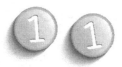

YOUR BROTHER CHUCK

If you want nice things, don't have kids. And if you want kids, don't have nice things.

Kids don't share your appreciation for the finer things in life. Mostly, they smear peanut butter and snot over everything you own.

And if you don't want orange antique sofas or orange oriental rugs or orange upholstered drapes, never, ever, ever buy Cheetos.

My advice: save your money on the good stuff until they are out of the house. (Caveat: you may not have a cent left to your name by then.)

One day we bought a new kitchen table. But I was wise to the destructive ways of my five little woodpeckers. Immediately, I called a glass company and ordered a thick piece of glass to cover the table and protect the wood surface.

I forgot my own advice. I had kids, yet I stupidly bought nice stuff.

I had it all set up; I was going to win this time. The kitchen table was to be delivered at noon. The glass, at two.

Except, the glass guy called and said he was running late. Apparently, the life of a glass guy is full of twists and turns and the unforeseen intrigue of an international spy.

Well, as unluck would have it, Katie had gotten a new pair of tap shoes that day. It turns out Katie discovered a new surface on which to try out her new tap shoes.

I came home to discover hundreds of pockmark dents on the surface of the new kitchen table when I distinctly remember ordering it nonpockmarked.

The glass arrived the next morning. My plan was not Katie-proof.

Years earlier, when I got a new car, I had a better plan. Fear.

The first week I had my new car, I was horrified to discover I had to let the kids get in it. Beth wanted to get in with an open soda can.

"Absolutely no, not in my new car. No."

"But I won't spill it, Daddy, I promise," which is always what they say right before they spill it, Daddy. I promise.

"I'm serious, Beth, I don't want my car to get all sticky and smelly. If you want to ride in a motorized litter box, let's take your mom's car."

"Please, Daddy, I promise I won't spill it."

"That's exactly what your brother Chuck said that one day."

Beth thought about that for a moment or two.

"We don't have a brother Chuck."

"Not anymore."

Beth thought about that for a moment two.

"We had a brother Chuck? What happened to him?"

"Let's just say he wishes he never spilled that soda in my last new car. I warned him."

Beth's eyes got wide. "Did you *kill* him?"

"Let's just say he wishes he never spilled that soda in my new car, and leave it at that."

She decided to leave the can of soda at home. So I decided to drive her to the birthday party.

On the way home, she threw up in my new car. That's when I discovered they had served cake with blue icing at that party.

THE DOLLAR HOT DOG NIGHT LESSON

One thing in particular my daughters always knew I would agree to do, no matter what, was to take them to see a Texas Rangers game.

A father-daughter day at the ballpark might be the sole reason to have kids. Watching baseball with your little girl, loading her up with snacks and stories of baseball lore, watching her do the Chicken Dance on the Jumbotron. Best thing ever.

I've been to thousands of Major League Baseball games and never once have come close to a foul ball. But on an August night in 2003, I caught a foul bat headed straight for Caroline. It was her ninth birthday and I got seats right behind the visitor's dugout. A nine-year-old doesn't have an appreciation for things like that, though. As Caroline once pointed out, "They sell ice cream at pretty much every seat in the ballpark, Dad, so who cares where you sit?"

In the middle of the game, the Rangers catcher, Einar Diaz, swung and missed and lost control of his bat. Suddenly, this heavy wooden slab of insta-lobotomization came spinning right toward Caroline. It was a killer souvenir.

I reached out and grabbed it right before it hit her head (truth be told, it would have landed in her lap, but saying it was going to hit her head made for a more heroic story to my wife), exhaled, then realized what I had caught, and handed the bat to Caroline, excited. "Look, you got a souvenir bat!"

"Big deal."

"You get to keep it."

"Who cares?"

"What a cool birthday gift."

"So what?"

"We just caught the most awesome souvenir ever. Lots of people catch foul balls, we caught a foul bat."

Caroline looked at me with all the joy of a Rasta on bath day and said coldly, "We're out of Starburst, Dad. You never bring enough Starburst."

Then she turned away in disgust. A bat?

Right then it occurred to me that Caroline was kidnap-proof. If someone snatched her, they'd return her after about twenty minutes with a huge note saying, "You can have her back. My condolences."

It wasn't like I saved her life or anything that night, but a flying baseball bat in the stomach sure would've hurt.

One night when Julie was eight, she and I went to a Rangers game and she loaded up on about fifteen red Super Ropes, which are these red thirty-four-inch-long ropes of red waxy red licorice. Did I mention they're red?

So were the vomit stains on my car's floor and my car's seats and my car's ceiling. So were the vomit stains on the kitchen floor and the stairs and her new bed sheets and her Cookie Monster pajamas. It even stained the kitchen countertop. So now we have two unusual souvenirs from baseball games.

Julie was an active volcano of Red Dye 40, which is the Red Dye Company's most spewy number.

Somehow that became my fault. As if I had forced her to eat fifteen Super Ropes.

But the most memorable game, and forgettable at the same time, happened one night when I had gotten home from work a bit late. Kelly ran up to me and asked if we could go to the game that night.

Of course we could.

Games start at 7:05. It was about 6:25. We had time to make it. And, it was a Wednesday. Every Wednesday is Dollar Hot Dog Night at Rangers Ballpark. All the way there we joked about how many hot dogs we were going to eat that night.

The final estimate was a thousand hot dogs. (When my kids were young and they'd ask me how much money I made, my stock answer was always a thousand dollars a year. They had no concept of money, so they had no idea what that meant. And, being in advertising, that was pretty accurate anyway. So at eight years old, Kelly realized that when I said we'd get a thousand hot dogs, that was a lot.)

Since it takes girls longer to do even the simplest thing, like hurry, we got to the ballpark a bit late. Kelly and I rushed to our seats, ready to buy our thousand hot dogs.

Just as we sat down, I spotted the hot dog vendor standing a few rows ahead of us, to our right. Facing the field, with his back to us, he was calling out to everyone, looking for takers, "HOT DOOOOOOOOGS. HOT DOOOOOOOOOOOGS."

I was a taker. I gave a little wave of the hand and said, "I'll take two."

"HOT DOOOOOOOOGS. HOT DOOOOOOOOOGS."

He must not have heard me. "I'll take two over here." I was still waving my hand, still wanting two hot dogs.

No response.

So I tried to assess the situation. I realized that, since he was a few rows in front of me, facing the field, he couldn't see my universally accepted "hey, over here, hot dog guy" gesture. What I needed was volume.

Realizing this was a teachable moment, I leaned over to my little sponge and said, "Sometimes in life, Kelly, to get what you want, you have to be assertive."

An I-have-no-idea-what-assertive-means look quickly spread across her face.

So I turned it up a notch. "I'LL TAKE TWO HOT DOGS. HEY, OVER HERE."

Assertive didn't work either. He walked a couple steps further down the section.

"HOT DOOOOOOOOGS. HOT DOOOOOOOOGS."

"I'LL TAKE TWO HOT DOGS OVER HERE."

"HOT DOOOOOOOOGS. HOT DOOOOOOOOGS."

Again, he ignored me, as if I were the '90s Corey Haim. Now I was getting a bit peeved. "HEY, I'LL TAKE TWO HOT DOGS OVER HERE."

Still nothing.

He had the audacity to walk down another row and call out again, "HOT DOOOOOOOOGS. HOT DOOOOOOOOGS."

I was failing miserably in my daughter's eyes at the one task I had set out to accomplish at that moment, which was buying two hot dogs, and no father wants to be put in that position.

I'd had enough.

"HEY, HOT DOG MAN, I WANT TWO HOT DOGS. WHAT THE HELL? ARE YOU GODDAMMED DEAF OR SOMETHING?"

Daggers.

Instantly, every single fan in our section turned and stared at me coldly, as if I actually *was* the guy who starred in the 1999 straight-to-video classic, *Demolition University*, and in unison they said, "Yes, as a matter of fact, he *is* deaf."

The hot dog guy reached the bottom of the section and turned to make his way back up the aisle. I saw a huge hearing aid device in his right ear.

I wanted to crawl under the seats, preferably with a hot dog in hand. But then my defense mechanism kicked in, and reason and logic took over.

"Wait a second," I said to anyone in the section who would acknowledge my existence, "who hires a deaf hot dog vendor? How come everyone else in this section knows he's deaf but me? Why isn't it printed on the ticket that you are in the Deaf Hot Dog Vendor section, just like they tell you when you are in the Obstructed Seating section or in the No Beer Drinking section? How many goddammed hot dogs can a deaf hot dog vendor actually sell? Isn't that bad for business? Are they hanging on to him because they're too afraid of the PR shit storm if they fire a deaf hot dog vendor? Did I ever tell you about the time I saved a little girl's life by catching a bat headed straight for her head?"

Kelly tugged on my shorts to get my attention. "Does assertive mean being mean to a deaf man, Daddy?"

"No."

"Then I'm telling Mommy you were mean to a deaf man."

Once he made eye contact with me, I ordered two hot dogs. I gave the guy a twenty. I told him to keep the change.

Lesson learned, Kelly. Lesson learned.

WHO WANTS GUM?

Most of being a father is having a good internal GPS.

I was in the basement of our house in Birmingham when I heard crying from far off. So I listened to where the crying was coming from and tracked it down to the garage.

But I didn't see anything.

So I headed toward the stairs, when I heard it again. A muffled whimpering. Wait a second, it *was* coming from the garage.

I followed the sound, which eventually led me to the trash can in the corner of the garage, where I saw two little legs sticking straight up. I was confused. Why would Ellen throw away a kid today? Trash pickup was still two days away.

I leaned over the trash can and pulled out the legs. They were attached to three-year-old Julie. I noticed a little step stool next to the trash can. She had fallen in headfirst.

"Julie, what are you doing?"

"Nothing."

"Why are you in the trash can?"

"I'm not."

"OK. Why *were* you in the trash can?"

"When?"

Then I noticed Julie was chewing gum. She loved gum. She loved gum so much that one of her favorite things to do was to find discarded wads of gum, pick them up and chew them. She figured, hey, free gum.

I was disgusted. "Are you chewing gum, Julie?"

"I don't know."

"Well, let me help you figure that out. Are your teeth moving up and down *on gum*?"

"I can't tell."

"Julie, did you spot a wad of gum in the trash can and reach in to get it and then fall in?"

She ran away crying. So I never learned the answer to my question.

1998

Five little ironers.

Dear Diary..." began the innocent-sounding note that Julie had written in what she figured would be her new diary, not realizing that what she was writing in was actually her dad's notebook for work. "Dear Diary: My dad..." Kevin read, prepared for a heartwarming glimpse into Julie's innermost thoughts about him. "Dear Diary: My dad, I think he is stoopid." With that, 1998 was off and running in the Sutton household. Mostly running.

CAROLINE: Mommy, do we have lots of kids?
ELLEN: Yes.
CAROLINE: Do we live in a shoe?

It was also a year most noted by being one in which Ellen gave birth to nothing. Although she did hatch a crazy notion or two. There was, however, one addition to the family. Shorty. A dog. Naturally, a female dog. Which Caroline quickly renamed Bonehead.

CAROLINE: Where are you taking Bonehead, Dad?
KEVIN: To obedience school.
CAROLINE: To school?
KEVIN: Yes, to school.
CAROLINE: Is Bonehead's teacher a person or a dog?

It will be remembered mostly as a year in which Ellen's Grand Plan to female-ize the world continued. It's worked well so far with Beth, Julie, and Kelly. (Ah, Julie, quite possibly Ellen's finest work, quite possibly the most female of all females in femaledom.) Caroline, Ellen is happy to report, is coming along well. At four years of age, she's proven a deftness of femaleness that belies her years. "Dad, how come I'm always right and you're always wrong?"

KEVIN:	Don't pick your nose, Caroline. It's disgusting.
CAROLINE:	I didn't, Dad.
KEVIN:	Then what is that on the end of your finger?
CAROLINE:	It's Katie's.

But, Ellen is sad to report, little two-year-old Katie still needs work. It's not that she isn't learning fluent Femaleish, it's just that she can't quite grasp the syntax.

KEVIN:	Katie, it's time for a nap.
KATIE:	If you don't know, then I'm not going to tell you.
KEVIN:	Katie, finish your dinner, please.
KATIE:	You care more about baseball than you do about me.
KEVIN:	Hey, Katie, you want to go for a walk?
KATIE:	You never listen to me.

Ellen is confident that, with a little fine-tuning, Katie will be a star pupil. She's only two. In fact, the same day she turned two (it was Valentine's Day if you're scoring at home), Beth broke her arm Rollerblading. She was in a cast for about eight weeks, missing the spring basketball and volleyball seasons. But, to Ellen's happiness, Beth didn't miss out on spring training for twelve-year-old females.

BETH:	(TO KELLY) I've found that girls are smarter than boys. But boys are smarter than dogs.

Ah, the passing of the baton. Perhaps there are no better keepers of the flame than Julie and Kelly, who have turned whining, lack of reason, and just plain stubbornness into an art form.

JULIE: I want to sleep on the top bunk, Daddy.

KELLY: No, *I* want to sleep on the top bunk.

JULIE: No, *I* want the top bunk.

KELLY: No, *I* want the top bunk.

(REPEAT THE ABOVE EXCHANGE SEVENTY-FOUR TIMES BEFORE CONTINUING.)

KEVIN: Knock it off, girls. You can't both sleep on the top bunk. Sorry, Julie, but it's Kelly's turn.

JULIE: You've never loved me. Ever. You always loved Kelly more.

KELLY: Hey, wait, you're going to make me sleep on the top bunk, Daddy? I could fall off and hurt myself. You're a bad daddy, Daddy.

JULIE: I want something for Christmas but I know you won't get me it.

KEVIN: What is it?

JULIE: I'm not going to tell you because I know you're not going to get it for me.

KEVIN: Well, how can I get it for you if you don't tell me what it is?

JULIE: OK. I want a fruit bat.

KEVIN: A fruit bat? Julie, we can't have a bat as a pet.

JULIE: See, I knew you wouldn't get it for me. You just don't love me.

So that was 1998 for the Suttons. Beth is twelve and in seventh grade. Julie and Kelly are nine, in fourth grade. Caroline is four. Katie is two. Ellen is busy taking five daughters into womanhood. And Kevin is simply trying to maintain some sense of perspective.

GUY AT WORK: So, five daughters, huh?

KEVIN: Yeah. It's not so bad, though. That means I have five little ironers. At least my pants will always be pressed.

As another year comes to an end, Kevin's family gathered to celebrate his mother's seventieth birthday. Kevin asked his mom if she felt old now that she turned seventy. "No," she responded, "I feel old because you're about to turn forty."

KEVIN: "Dear Diary: My mom, I think she is crool."

Merry Christmas to all our friends, from Kevin, Ellen, Beth, Julie, Kelly, Caroline, and Katie Sutton.

And to our Jewish friends, we'd like to say Happy Hanukkah. And to our African friends, we'd like to say Happy Kwanzaa. And to our Muslim friends, we'd like to say quit bombing our buildings.

1999

Wednesday, December 15, 1999. Day 6,027 in captivity.

After sixteen and a half years of marriage and five daughters (two of them being fathered by Kevin—Beth and one of the twins), people think Kevin must have ascertained some special insight into women that he can pass along to others. Some sage piece of universal wisdom. Some never-before-noted observation. As if being constantly exposed to dangerously high decibel levels of shrill hysteria and shrieking would somehow actually sharpen one's senses, or could possibly make keener one's ability to focus and concentrate. Like gunmakers who choose to remain unaware of the damage their products inflict, Kevin, co-manufacturer of five fine custom females, refuses to be held accountable for the impact his products have on society. A gun, like a woman, is an unpredictable weapon. Especially when loaded. Sad to say, in sixteen and a half years, Kevin has learned very little about the "fairer sex." Only that they're never fair, and there's never...well, strike that last train of thought. Anyway, in all those years, about the only constant he can see is their uncanny ability to cry at any given moment. Young or old, happy or sad, rich or poor, gaping head wound or nongaping head wound, pretty much all women do is cry. There are only three things which make a man cry: 1) Death of a family member. 2) Death of a dog. 3) *Field of Dreams.* By contrast, and as part of the requirements of the Nobel Peace Prize application process, here is a list of the things that make a woman cry:* a sad song, a sad book, wheat, a big fluffy towel, a balloon, happiness, rain, velvet, a forty-five-watt-or-higher light bulb, math, sand, paper, sandpaper, spiders, having their toes accidentally run over by your car (look, I said it was an accident, and besides, there were no broken bones, and besides, get out of the way next time), lettuce, any of the elements in the periodic table, especially sulfur (who knew?), meat, meat by-products, *Once and Again*, thighs, any flower girl at any wedding, milk, Ginger Spice going out on her own, paint, the threat of a restraining order, midgets, butter (includes margarine and other cooking fats made of refined vegetable oils processed to a similar consistency, often churned with pasteurized skim milk, and generally fortified with vitamins A and D), *Love Is...* (a comic strip about two little naked eight-year-olds who aren't even married), and the following three statements: 1) "I love you." 2) "You complete me." 3) "Yes, as a matter of fact, those pants do make you look fat, but it's really not fair to blame the pants; they'd probably look good on someone else."** With all that crying, no wonder Earth is two-thirds water. By the way, Beth is thirteen and in eighth grade. Julie and Kelly are ten, going on four, and in fifth grade. Caroline is five, in kindergarten. Katie is three and just plain cute. Ellen is thirty-eight and no longer employed (she was downsized, but please, no weight jokes, Kevin found those don't work [see list above]), and Kevin is forty and slowly going deafer but, oddly, happier.

Merry Christmas from Kevin, Ellen, Beth, Julie, Kelly, Caroline, and Katie Sutton.

*Legal disclaimer one: the preceding is not meant to be comprehensive, as such a list would be logistically impossible to compile.

**Legal disclaimer two: honesty is not always the best policy.

2000

Our own little solar system.

Certain days in human history are so defining, not only are they forever etched in our collective memories, but they change the course of mankind from that moment forward. July 4, 1776, is the day the Declaration of Independence was signed. January 20, 2000, is the day Ken Griffey Jr. was signed by the Reds. Those dates roll off the memory's tongue as easily as a forty-one-year-old man rolls out of bed when, let's say, the morning's alarm is sounding and a foreign elbow sharply and repeatedly jabs him in the side of the vulnerable and mostly unprotected rib cage, inviting him to kindly get up and turn off the alarm. But few realize the historical significance that recently occurred on December 7, 2000. For it was on this watershed day that Kevin Sutton, astronaut in a strange universe, became the first man to see the surface of the sun and live to tell about it. It happened like this. Kevin and Ellen had just arrived back home from Kevin's company's Christmas party. Ellen, it seems, had come back from the party with considerably more wine inside her than when she left. (For the record, she left with none in her.) Now, so as not to project the wrong idea, Ellen rarely finds herself in this situation. Only four times in her (married) life, in fact. While those four times produced the five wonderful offspring Kevin and Ellen so proudly share, this night produced something different. This night produced clarity. While Ellen lay in bed, with visions of fermented grapes dancing in her head, she looked up and uttered the words that took Kevin into new and uncharted territory. *"The room is spinning around me."* Hidden within what seemed like the innocent ramblings of a slightly inebriated wife were the nuggets of truth that all wives—all women—carry deep within them, and which Ellen had finally, accidentally, let slip out. "Let me get this straight," Kevin prodded. "Did you just admit what I think you just admitted?" *"Uh,"* Ellen responded, suspecting Kevin was onto a line of questioning that could be incriminating. Kevin continued: "When you say the room is spinning around you, are you finally, after seventeen years of marriage, admitting that the entire world does, indeed, really revolve around you?" The trade secret finally out, Ellen recoiled in horror at the thought of the reprimand she would be receiving from the International Female Tribunal. Then she fell asleep and forgot about it all. By the next morning life was normally abnormal in the Sutton household. The planets were realigned. Five little orbs happily revolving around the mother sun, while astronaut Kevin tries in vain to explore new civilizations and boldly go where no man has gone before. <u>Planet Caroline</u>. You know your child is watching too much TV when she asks, as little six-year-old Caroline recently asked Ellen, "Mommy, can you wake me up tomorrow at eight o'clock, seven central?" Recently, with the family sitting around the dinner table, Kevin was looking over Caroline's daily behavior sheet from school, and was dismayed to discover she had gotten written up for yelling in class. (Apparently, the progressive school systems are outlawing yelling at the first-grade level now.) "What is this behavior check all about, Caroline? It says you were yelling in class today." *"No, Dad, it wasn't me. The teacher made a mistake."* Hmmm, he'd never heard that one before. "What do you mean she made a mistake?" *"It wasn't me who was the one yelling in class, Dad. It was a boy in my class named Sutton Caroline."* "Wait a minute. There is a boy in your class named Sutton Caroline?" *"Yes, Dad."* "That is an amazing coincidence, Caroline." *"That's what I thought, too. And he was the one yelling in class."* "But how come you got blamed for it?" *"You know how if your name is Caroline Sutton then the teacher has your name down in her book as Sutton Caroline? Well, when my teacher went to mark his name down for yelling in class, she looked down at her list and instead of marking down Sutton Caroline, who is the boy who was really yelling, she accidentally marked down my name, Caroline Sutton, who is the girl who wasn't really yelling."* By this time, Caroline's sisters were incredulous. Is Dad actually buying this unbelievable line of crap? No, not buying, just window shopping. "So let me get this straight. Your teacher made a mistake?" *"Yes, Dad."* "That's not right, Caroline. You should not get in trouble for something you did not do. I'll tell you what, first thing tomorrow, I am going to meet with your teacher and tell her what really happened." *"Oh, you can't do that, Dad. She is getting married tomorrow."* "Wait, I thought she already got married." *"It didn't take, Dad, she has to get married again."* "In the middle of the week? That is unusual, Caroline." *"That's what I thought, Dad."* "Okay, then I will give this Sutton Caroline's parents a call right now to let them know what happened." *"Oh, Dad, you can't do that either. Sutton Caroline is on vacation in California for the next two weeks. They left after school."* "Wow, he must have incredibly nice parents to take him out of school in the middle of the semester for vacation." *"Yeah, that's what I thought, too, Dad. It must be nice to have nice parents."* Then she flashed Kevin her I-wish-I-had-nice-parents smile, and left the table. And that is the Sutton Caroline story. Not only is Caroline creative, she shows signs of mastering advanced levels of physics. One astute observation she made during one of her highly scientific experiments had to do with mass and density, performed in the lab in the back seat of the minivan. "Dad, why does a booger feel so much bigger in your nose than it is on your finger?" Precisely the path a young Albert Einstein began his long and storied career on. Can a Nobel Prize be far away? Kevin and Ellen anxiously await the call from MIT. One Saturday, Caroline came home from her soccer game and said: *"Dad, guess what? I scored sixty-seven goals today."* Not that Kevin would doubt his little daughter's considerable talents, but this from a girl who has a self-imposed restraining order against the ball—she must stay at least a hundred feet away from it at all times. Later Caroline admitted the truth. It turns out it wasn't quite sixty-seven goals at all. It was, in fact, zero. "Why'd you tell me you scored sixty-seven goals?" Kevin asked her. *"I just wanted you to love me,"* Caroline said. The ability to unleash guilt on command is innate in the species. As evidenced by the day Kevin took Katie to run some errands, which included a stop at Toys"R"Us and the ice cream store. He didn't take Caroline along (let's just say she wasn't in the running errands and stopping at Toys"R"Us and the ice cream store mood). Later that night, after dinner, Caroline approached Kevin, holding a piece of paper with a cute little map of their neighborhood she'd drawn. She smiled and said sweetly, *"Dad, I drew a map for you."* "Thanks," said Kevin. *"A MAP OF EVERYTHING YOU DID WRONG!"* Caroline shot back. Then she shoved it into his gut, which is vulnerable and mostly unprotected, and stormed out of the room with her hands firmly on her hips. Planet Julie. If Caroline is destined for a distinguished career in physics, Julie is on target to be a well-accomplished diplomat. She came down for dinner one day, looked at Kevin and said, "I just noticed, you're kinda ugly, Dad." When the Suttons got back from spring break in Arizona, Kevin, who was known to be kinda ugly, noticed a piece of paper taped to the front door. On it, in Julie's sixth-grade scrawl, was written: "DEAR ROBBERS: WE ARE GONE ON VACATION, PLEASE DO NOT STEAL ANYTHING." When Kevin pointed out to Julie that this was perhaps not the smartest thing to do, Julie reminded him, "Nothing got stolen, did it?" Philosopher Julie. Diplomat Julie. Lucky Julie. Planet Beth. Beth is in her first year of high school. Just six more years left. She's typical of other ninth-grade girls. She goes to the mall with her friends, stays up late talking on the phone, spends way too much time on the Internet, and convinces boys to dress up in women's clothing. One night Beth called and asked Kevin to bring her camera to a friend's house. It seems there was a picture "she just had to take." To his horror, when Kevin arrived he saw some of the boys at the party were dressed in women's formal wear. "We thought it would be funny, and they actually did it," was Beth's response. (Q: At what age do they begin robbing you of your dignity? A: Fourteen.) Kevin noticed one boy was enjoying caressing his balloons. Kevin warned him, "Don't have too much fun with those things; otherwise, you are going to have to buy yourself a house and a car." He turned redder than the cute little Italian pumps he was wearing. Beth had a bad baggage year. Aside from having her luggage stolen at church camp, she also had her luggage lost forever on her return flight from Arizona. Without naming airlines, Kevin will offer a hint: when you call up the American Airlines website on the Internet, don't be surprised if your computer crashes. Planet Kelly. Kelly, like Julie, is in sixth grade. Kelly, like Julie, is eleven. Kelly, like Julie, looks just like Julie. A point we had to remind her of recently.

Kelly said, "Julie, you're ugly." Ellen said, *"But Kelly, she looks just like you."* Kelly said, "Oh, yeah." But mostly Kelly wants to be an actress. One day, she wanted to go see a movie really badly that was rated R. Ellen didn't want her to see it just as really badly. After hours of crying, Kelly cleared her head and came up with a sane, rational reason why Ellen should reconsider: "Mom, you know I want to be an actress. If you let me go see this movie, I'll see all the bad stuff the actresses are doing and I'll know not to do those things when I'm in a movie. Seeing it will help me be a better actress." Clever, yes. Convincing, no. (Dear Kelly: I have learned the hard way that when your mom says no, she means no. Love, Dad.) <u>Planet Katie.</u> And finally we come to our Pluto. Our little Katie, age four. Perhaps the wisest of the bunch. Katie sits there, takes it all in, and dispenses her own unique, uncommon brand of humor and wisdom. Katie on material wealth: "Katie, if you could have just one thing in the world, what would it be?" asked Kevin. *"The world,"* she replied. Katie on politics: "Katie, why did you vote for George Bush (at her preschool election) instead of Al Gore?" *"Those were the only choices we had."* Katie on meteorology: *"If it wasn't so hot, I wouldn't be so hot."* Katie on family: *"We have a really itchy family, don't we?"* Katie on sharing: *"If you give it to me, I won't have to take it from you."* And, finally, Katie on the holidays: *"Daddy, why does everyone have weddings at Christmas?"* "What are you talking about?" *"People always say, 'Marry Christmas, everyone.'"*

Marry Christmas, everyone. From Kevin, Ellen, Beth, Julie, Kelly, Caroline, and Katie. The Sutton Universe. And to Sutton Caroline, we will talk to your parents when you get back from California.

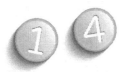

EXPLAINING THE KARDASHIANS

Try as you might, there are certain things you just cannot explain to kids. So don't even bother.

Here is a brief list:

Why her teacher has to live in a cardboard refrigerator box in an empty lot behind the school, while the Kardashians get to live in a mansion on TV.

Rap music.

Why God created bad men and how those men can be bad their whole lives, but if right before they die they tell God they are sorry, they get to go to heaven.

Why she is not allowed to hit Caroline who is the most annoying big sister ever as much as she wants to hit Caroline, and then just say she is sorry and get to go to heaven or to the ice cream store.

Logic. And heaven.

Why she has to choose between human or dancer.

The randomness of radio airplay.

What that vibrating rubber Fudgsicle under Mommy's side of the bed is.

Why she should go wash her hands right now.

But the most impossible one of all to explain to kids is what it means when the power goes out. Most adults who work at the electric company don't get the concept, so why should my girls?

"Daddy, the stupid TV stopped TVing."

"Well, that's because the power's out."

"Oh, OK. Turn the TV back on."

"The power's out."

"OK. Then turn on the TV so we can watch something while the power's out."

"Uh, I can't. There is no power, you know, no electricity. The TV runs on electricity that comes through that socket thingy on the wall that I always have to yell at you not to stick your fingers into or else you will end up with pro football brain. Well, that electricity is no longer coming through those holes, so we don't have the power needed to run the TV. Do you understand?"

"Yes, we're not stupid, Dad. Now, can you turn the TV back on?"

"Look, for the tenth time, I cannot turn on the TV. There is no power right now. When the electric company gets the power back up and running, you can watch TV again."

"Well then, can we—"

"You cannot watch a movie, or play a video game, or get on the computer either."

Silence, as the ice forms on their hearts.

"You are the meanest dad ever."

"Wait, a few months ago you got me a coffee mug that said World's Greatest Dad. You can't take that back. That's official."

"It should have said World's Stupidest Fat-Head Meanest Dad."

"Do you want to be grounded from watching TV?"

"What's the point of that, Einstein? The TV isn't working. Haven't you noticed?"

At that point, you realize the electric chair isn't a workable alternative right now either. So you walk away muttering. Get used to that. Walking away muttering happens a lot.

Oh, and kids don't get the concept of time change either. Good luck with that one.

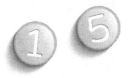

NINE LIVES

I don't like the smell of cat pee.

There, I admit it. I don't want to give anyone the false impression that I do. And, if that makes you think differently about me, then sorry. But, unlike my wife and daughters, who seem to find the smell of cat pee invigorating, I don't.

I've had friends ask me, "Why have you never invited me to your home?" To which I answer, "If you want to see what my house is like, just find the nearest litter box and bury your head in it. Oh, and I'd leave your wallet someplace safe."

I don't hate cat pee because I am a dog person and not a cat person. Frankly, dog pee isn't all that pleasant either. Nor is kid pee.

But when our cat pees in the house, mainly I want to kill it. Maybe it's because when our cat pees in the house, it's on my shoes, on my pillow, on my gym bag, on my coat, on my computer bag, even on my computer. The cat pees on everything mine, all the time.

Often I find myself Googling "More than one way to skin a cat." In times like these I have discovered that Google isn't the be-all and end-all it claims to be.

When my daughter Beth graduated from college and got an apartment, she made the unfortunate decision to get a cat, and the even more unfortunate decision to get this particular cat.

As is always the case with first-time cat owners, it wasn't long before she regretted her decision.

This mentally challenged cat never learned the whole litter box thing. Beth would come home to an apartment reeking of cat pee. She realized she had to get rid of that thing.

For some reason, she thought she should get rid of it on us. As if they didn't have fifty-five-gallon drums of wild coyotes in Georgia where she was living.

So she made the twelve-hour drive home to dump her cat-peeing cat on us. For some odd reason, my youngest daughter, Katie, fell in love with the thing. Almost a creepy sort of cat lady love. She has taken more than ten thousand pictures of this cat, created its own Facebook page, and treats it like a thing that shouldn't be dropped into a fifty-five-gallon drum of wild coyotes.

Before we go any further, I need to point out, I am a huge hater of animal cruelty. I love animals; I believe wholeheartedly in the SPCA and what it is doing to rescue and care for animals.

But just because I don't believe in the death sentence doesn't mean what we did to bin Laden wasn't the right thing to do.

This is the bin Laden of cats.

One day, I had just had it. I was on my way to the airport for a week away on business when I decided this cat had to go. It had peed on my luggage. My plan was to drop it off in a field somewhere between our house and the airport, and let it live its life in cat-urinating freedom. I also dropped off a bowl of food (hey, I'm not a monster).

I guess the field was a bit too close to our house because, six days later, that darn cat found its way back home. I honestly don't know how that cat did it.

(Did the cat bring back the bowl? Of course not. That cat made me have to lie to my wife and tell her I didn't, in fact, know what happened to her little yellow bowl. I hate that cat.)

Look, I am not proud of what I did. Not dropping off that cat far enough for it never to find its way home is something I will have to live with for the rest of my life.

Since this cat won't run away on its own and won't find a vat of wild coyotes to play in, I have come up with a genius idea.

I am going to teach it to text.

Texting is a sure-fire way to get yourself killed. I wrote an antitexting and driving billboard campaign that shows an overturned car with the headline: "I M DED." A second billboard had a picture of a woman's mangled face next to the headline: "M I HOT?"

I also wrote an antitexting commercial that was killed because it was controversial. It had a cop pulling over a driver who had been weaving all over the highway. The cop asks the driver if she had been texting. The driver responds, "No, officer, I swear I wasn't texting, I'm just really drunk." The cop stares her down and says, "OK, get out of here, but I had better not catch you texting." Then we'd bring up a line that says, "Texting and driving is five times more distracting than drinking and driving." I thought that was a pretty powerful way to get people to reframe texting and driving in their minds. Like with most government clients, though, they want advertising that people think is cute, not advertising anyone responds to. They ran with the Timmy the No-Text Turtle commercial.

I am going to teach this cat to text in hopes that, next time it is driving to the spa or to the convenience store, it will get the urge to start texting with its other cat buddies, run off the road, and die in a fiery car crash.

That way, its ultimate demise will be from its own paw, and not mine.

Oh, and I need to teach it to drive.

Fatherhood is one part sperm, ninety-nine parts inspiration.

THE COOKIE JAR INCIDENT

Being a father of daughters is a matter of outsmarting them. Little girls will always try to get away with something. But you have the advantage. The advantage being that kids are inherently stupid.

Kids think they are smart. And that is the key to their downfall. Jerry Jones thinks he knows football. The Dallas Cowboys are Yesterday's Team.

Life for kids started the day they were born. They are under the mistaken belief that that's when life for you started as well.

Kids are naïve enough to think that the crap they are trying to pull on you is the first time in the history of crap-pulling that that crap is being pulled.

They are totally clueless to the fact that they inherited your crap-pulling gene. You've done it all before.

Having twins just means you have to shovel twice as much of that crap.

We had a cookie jar that was a ceramic figurine of Tommy from *Rugrats*. His hat was the lid. My girls loved *Rugrats*. And they loved cookies.

They loved cookies so much that Ellen decided it was time to move the cookie jar from the counter to the top of the refrigerator.

The twins did not like that development in their cookie-snatching routine. So they hatched a plan. It was the kind of plan that maybe might have worked the first time it was tried, maybe back when Adam and Eve's son Jesus tried to pull it on them or something.

But I was wise to what was happening. Mainly because, like I said, I've been there.

So, I was in the kitchen eating a sandwich when Kelly, who was six, came up to me with the sweetest expression on her face. Clue one.

The fact that she didn't have a clump of Julie's hair in her hand or wasn't screeching like a raptor in heat was a dead giveaway that something was amiss. Clue two.

Kelly walked into the living room, about twenty feet from me, and called out in a feeble attempt to strike up a conversation—an adult, coherent conversation. Or at least her version of what that might me. But mostly it was an attempt to get me out of the kitchen. Clue three, you're out.

"Hey, Daddy, what's up?"

"Just eating a sandwich."

"Can you come in here? I want to show you something."

"OK." I'm thinking, she's six. Other than a new booger, what could she possibly have to show me that I haven't already seen? I mean, everything she has, we gave her.

I wanted to see how she was going to play this. I gathered up my sandwich and walked into the living room.

"What's up, Kelly-Kel?" I asked.

She thought for a moment about something to say. Finally, a thought arrived. Well, it was more like a syllable.

"Uh, hey." She stared at me for a while without saying anything, then smiled.

Ah, I said to myself, she's attempting the old Diversion Ploy. I remember the first time I executed that, back in 1968, when I asked my mom if it looked like the tires on the car were flat, and when she went to look I sneaked a "pet" snake into the house that I had found down at the creek.

Slidey was my pet snake for all of seventeen minutes. I loved that snake.

But after less than five minutes at this game, Kelly was already running out of plays. She looked at me again and said, "Uh, hey, Daddy. How are things?"

"Fine."

Then I heard it.

Kkkkkkkkkkrchhhhhhhhhhhhhh. Kkkrchhhhhhhhhhhhhhh. Kkkkkkkkkkrchhhhhhhhhhhhhhh.

It was the unmistakable sound of wood on tile, of a kitchen chair being slowly pushed across a kitchen floor. I first heard this sound in the winter of 1965, and wood on tile audiology hasn't changed a bit since.

Kelly heard it too. But she wasn't letting on.

Kkkkkkkkkkrchhhhhhhhhhhhhhh. Kkkkkkkkkkhhhhhhhhhhhh. Kkkkkkkkkkrchhhhhhhhhhhhhhh.

From the living room, I could make out the trajectory of the kitchen chair. It was heading from position six at the kitchen table, toward the counter next to the refrigerator, at a forty-seven-degree angle—the counter that would be a perfect stepping-stone for a six-year-old to stand on in order to get to a cookie jar.

Like the Tell-Tale Heart, Kelly's conscience was starting to eat away at her. I could tell she had an inkling that I had heard what was going on in the kitchen. So she pulled out all the stops.

"So, Daddy. I have a question. You and Mommy, are you serious?"

"Uh, yeah, Kelly. I think it's going to last. I am glad you care enough to ask me that sort of thing. A question that caring deserves a cookie. Let me get you one."

"NO, DADDY! I HATE COOKIES."

And a Catholic priest hates reading *Boys Life*.

So I headed straight toward the cookie jar and was shocked, I mean *shocked*, to see Julie standing on the kitchen chair, just about to climb onto the counter to grab and take down the cookie jar.

Julie froze. "Kelly made me do it."

Right after she threw Kelly under the bus, she took that bus up to her bedroom, crying. Kelly followed her, also crying, with fresh bus-tire marks.

It was time to be a dad. I went to their room to dole out the discipline.

I knocked on their door. Nobody answered. It was the old Maybe Dad Will Think We're At Work Technique.

I didn't fall for it; they were only six. I entered their room and the twins were hiding in their bunk beds. The kid-sized lumps under the covers were a dead giveaway.

I approached Julie.

"Julie, I am very disappointed in you."

She peeked out her head from under the covers.

"I'm sorry, Daddy."

"You should be sorry. If you are going to move the kitchen chair, next time put a kitchen towel under each leg to muffle the sound. You might want to wrap a rubber band around them to help them stay on. Do that, and your mom will never be able to hear the chair scoot across the floor next time you want a cookie."

A dad has to be willing to do the dirty work and be a father when the situation calls for it.

MY FATHER THE HERO

Every father wants his daughter to look up to him as this bigger-than-life figure. Growing up, Julie was often so thoughtful to point out just how much bigger I was getting around the waist part of me. But hey, you take what you can get.

Your kids look up to you for so many things. Nearly every one of those things is related to you giving them your money. But those rare times when you can be more than an ATM machine to them are special.

There was a day at the mall when I was with Katie that stands out as one such moment, when she realized her dad was more than a dad. He was a hero.

I am not sure exactly what caused me to act that day. I was tired, pissed off at humanity, and not in a particularly caring mood to give a damn about anyone or anything.

Yes, it was the holiday season.

Sometimes I wonder if I did what I did simply as a way to show off in front of my littlest daughter. Would I have risen to the occasion and been so bold, acted so quickly, and saved so many lives that day had I not had the specter of failure in her eyes looming over me?

In the quiet moments, any hero wonders whether what he did was one-time dumb luck, or if he truly has it in him to do it again, should the moment arise.

Going to the mall during the holidays is a joyless, frustrating experience that starts with the bumper-to-bumper traffic just to get to a grossly overcrowded parking lot where angry, beaten-down drivers desperately fight for that one available space nobody can seem to locate. Then, when you finally do park some six miles away, you have to slog your way into a carnival of Tommy Hilfiger-shirt-wearers screaming at their bratty kids.

Happy holidays.

By the time you get what you want, you hate humanity and everything it stands for.

So nobody could have blamed me if I didn't act that day. Not a single soul would have thought any less of me had I just allowed myself to be one of the victims.

But some days you just say, enough is enough. And that day I refused to be a victim.

Katie and I were done shopping for the day and were heading home, exhausted. All we wanted to do was fight our way out of the morass.

The crowd to the down escalator reminded me of one of those Japanese subway stops where thousands of commuters are shoved and squeezed through the tiny subway doors.

We were sardines, and our can was the narrow escalator opening. The extremely large woman in front of me, to complete the metaphor, smelled of dead oily fish. And talk about morass, she had more ass than any three women should have.

Katie and I finally squeezed on. I held her hand tightly for fear that she would get lost in this Pacific Ocean of humanity.

We had gone maybe two feet when disaster struck. The escalator stopped, dead in its tracks.

We were trapped on an escalator that wasn't moving. Our worst fears came true.

Instantly, panic ensued. Blind, out-of-control panic. Women screamed. Children cried. Men called out to Jesus to take them to heaven that very moment and spare them the agony of the inevitable slow, painful death. People phoned family members and said their last good-byes.

But I didn't want to die in that mall. I didn't even like being alive in a mall, so the prospect of dying in one was unacceptable.

I saw fear in Katie's eyes. I couldn't stand seeing that, and I knew I couldn't live with myself if I let something happen to her.

So I sprang into action.

By my calculations, nearly fifty people were stuck on that escalator. They were scared and desperate. I told myself that I couldn't let them die. Not here. Not today. Not on my watch (I had dropped my watch and the fat lady in front of me was standing on it).

I have often heard of a ninety-pound woman finding some divine power to lift a two-ton car off her baby, and that inspiration swept through me. I took over.

I told the trapped victims that if they wanted to get out of this alive, the first thing they needed to do was to act like they were on a flight of stairs. Just put one foot in front of the other and they could walk down to freedom.

Somehow, it worked. I was able to talk nearly fifty shaken, scared holiday shoppers off a jammed escalator and onto the safety of the floor below us.

Even though people heralded me as a hero, I think the fact that it was the holidays exaggerated the situation. I heard the local paper wanted to write a story about me. But it wasn't about me. The look of pride in Katie's eyes was all the reward I needed.

I didn't need praise. I didn't need press. I didn't need to be fitted for a cape.

What I really didn't need, though, was Katie saying to her mom when we got home, "Daddy screamed at a fat lady on the escalator in the mall."

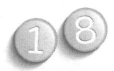

THERE'S MORE THAN ONE WAY
TO BUTTER A CAT

Ellen and I were at a dinner party when the subject, naturally, turned to how to get rid of your cat.

I had mentioned my story about dropping off the cat miles from our house in hopes that it would find a new life among other non-urination-savvy animals, and about my utter consternation of how the damn thing managed to make its way back home to Katie.

In the darkest of times, in the most surprising of places, you are always reminded of the inherent goodness of people. And this night, at this dinner party, was no exception. In the middle of this horrifying display of wealth and abundance, one humanitarian woman, a total stranger, offered a tip I had never heard before.

She told me that if I really truly want to make sure a cat doesn't find its way back home, take it far away and, instead of just dropping off the urinary terrorist, first cover its paws in butter.

Butter. (Yeah, I thought that was crazy too.)

Immediately, I feigned a sudden illness so I could race home to my computer to Google this craziness and get started on the process.

Surely I was being duped. But, no. When I Googled "Cats paw in butter," I was surprised to find a number of entries. This thing was for real.

I tried to find out the explanation or the origin of such a bizarre act. Best I got was that a cat will call home anywhere it cleans itself, and as it licks off all that butter, it is confused into thinking that very spot is home.

I don't care how the science works, just as long as it works.

As I have always tried to teach my girls, don't take things at face value; always try to find a better way.

So I thought about this smothering-a-cat's-paws-in-butter trick. And I thought of a better way.

Sure, you cover its paws in butter, but why not then sprinkle on a little cinnamon? Wouldn't that make it much more mouthwatering to coyotes?

Yeah, that's what I thought too.

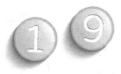

WHAC-A-KID

Getting five girls to bed every night is basically like playing that arcade game called Whac-A-Mole.

I'd spend roughly an hour or two desperately trying to pound their heads with a mallet to get them to go down and stay down. But randomly they would pop back up and challenge me to whack them back down.

Between requests for water, requests to go to the bathroom, and requests for wanting a sister to die immediately, they never stayed down for long.

Beth was easy to get to go to sleep, because Beth was always easy to deal with. You asked her to go to sleep, she went to sleep, like any nondefective child would do.

Caroline and Katie were like wild monkeys on crack, bouncing off the ceiling and jumping from bed to bed. But once you got the restraining harnesses on, all you had to do was sing them a song or two, read them a book, or threaten them with eternal life on the rap circuit, and they'd be out like a light.

Julie and Kelly? That was a different story. I'd bribe them, plead with them, yell at them, promise to buy them shiny new cars on their tenth birthdays, but they wouldn't go to sleep. Sleeping meant wasting valuable fighting time.

One night, after reading and singing to them, I thought I had finally gotten them to sleep. I tiptoed out of the room and quietly closed the door behind me. I had scaled Mount Everest once more. Sir Edmund Hillary had nothing on me.

From experience, though, I knew not to walk away too far. Kids do not realize they are creatures of habit, and I knew the habits of these creatures.

Like clockwork, I heard someone say something. Then I heard someone say something back, a bit louder. Then I heard someone say something back to that, even louder. Then came the crying. God, how I hated the crying.

So I trudged back in the room. Kelly was bawling uncontrollably.

"OK, what happened?" That is the kind of question a father legally has to ask, even though he really doesn't give a damn at all about the answer.

Kelly was crying so hard she could barely form words. Her lip was quivering and she was shaking with convulsions: "Ju-Ju-Ju-Julie ca-ca-ca-ca-called m-m-m-m-m-me a b-b-b-b-b-b-boy."

"What?"

To be clear, I wasn't asking "What?" as in "What did you say? I did not hear you"; I was asking "What?" as in "What the hell is wrong with you kids?"

Kelly chose A from above. She thoughtfully repeated herself: "Ju-Ju-Ju-Julie ca-ca-ca-ca-called m-m-m-m-m-me a b-b-b-b-b-b-boy."

"She called you a boy?"

"Y-y-y-y-yes."

"And that's why you're crying?"

"Y-y-y-y-yes. Be-be-be-because I'm *not* a b-b-b-boy."

"She didn't hit you or kick you or bite you or sever your spleen? She just called you a boy?"

That was a new one.

Meanwhile, Julie had been stone cold silent up in the top bunk. Which meant she was guilty as sin. Still, I had to ask her, "Julie, did you call Kelly a boy?"

"No."

"L-l-l-l-lying liar."

"No, I did not. I did not call her a boy."

I could see this was going nowhere. It was too late for logic (with girls, logic's bedtime is typically 7:15 a.m.), but that was all I had at the moment.

So I asked her, "Kelly, are you a boy?"

"No."

"Julie, is Kelly a boy?"

"No."

"OK, then. That's settled. Kelly, you are not a boy. Girls, go to sleep."

Kelly calmed down. I guess knowing she would not one day magically drop a pair of testicles has that effect on a girl.

I turned to exit their room. But, once again, they were not smart enough to figure out what I did so many other nights.

Their room has a weird little jut by the door, which creates a strange wall that I can hide behind so they can't tell that I'm still in the room.

So I would walk to the door, turn out the light, loudly open the door, make loud footstep sounds as if I was leaving the room, and then loudly close the door, knowing they would think I was gone. Then I'd stand in their room, silently, in the dark, ready to catch them in the act of fighting. I pulled this trick about a million times.

After waiting a few seconds to be certain I was long gone down the hallway and out of earshot, Julie whispered to Kelly, "Boy."

"I am not a boy!" Kelly insisted.

"You are too a—" Julie didn't get the insult all the way formed before I flipped on the light and caught her red-handed.

"Julie, didn't I tell you not to call your sister a boy?"

I don't know what made Julie burst into tears. That I nailed her in the act, or that I somehow magically appeared in their room when she was certain I was long gone, which scared her into thinking her dad must be a ghost.

I left and went downstairs. Ellen was watching TV. She asked why Julie was crying.

"Because Kelly's not a boy."

2001

Caroline declares Jihad on the truth.

Some children are gifted in math. Others are gifted in the arts. Still others have latent, subtle gifts that may not be apparent but are present nonetheless. Then there's the case of Caroline Sutton. Like *The Shining*, she has a gift. A paranormal gift. The gift for, we will say politely, bending the truth. OK, not really bending it, more like twisting it. OK, not really twisting it. More like double knotting once, then adding a slipknot, then a triple knot, then a weave, then cauterizing the ends so it's forever fused in a mangled, tangled mess with no beginning and no end. *That* kind of bending the truth. It's a gift she freely and unselfishly shares with Kevin and Ellen on a daily basis. This isn't just the simple garden-variety, "I didn't bite my sister and you can't prove that those teeth marks on her back are mine or that the hunks of skin in my braces are hers" kind of truth bending as practiced by Kevin and Ellen's four other giftless children. No, this is the stuff of legend. Kevin and Ellen are happy to report that Caroline is in the second grade, but fabricating at an eleventh-grade level. The major political science universities are already sending scouts to recruit her. A scholarship cannot be far away, especially considering the following exchange: "Dad, I need a new pair of shoes." *"No, you don't."* "Yes, my teacher said I can't come to school tomorrow unless I have a new pair of shoes." *"Your teacher didn't tell you that."* "Yes, she did." *"Well, I'll call her and ask."* "Wait a minute, Dad. You know what I was just thinking? It wasn't my teacher, it was another teacher. A teacher whose name I don't know." *"Well, I'll get out the school directory and you can show me what she looks like."* "She's a new teacher, Dad, she just started yesterday. So she's not in the directory." By this time, Kevin was starting to get a little suspicious, the same way he's starting to believe that maybe O. J. really is guilty. *"OK, that makes it easy, then. Tomorrow I'll just ask the principal who the new teacher is and then I'll go ask her why she told you that you needed new shoes."* "Wait a minute, Dad. You know what I was just thinking? It wasn't a teacher at all. It was a parent." *"Oh, then I'll get out the parent directory* (Kevin had her this time, ha-ha-ha—there is no parent directory) *and we'll see who it is."* "Look, Dad, what's it matter who told me? The point is, someone told me. I don't remember if it was a lady or a man, or if it was at school or not. But someone told me I need new shoes for school. SO GET ME NEW SHOES."* Caroline then thrust her hands on her hips and wagged her head, a move known in mind-wrestling circles as a Full Ellen. Turns out, Caroline had to make a diorama for school and she needed a shoe box, and she simply didn't like the shoe boxes we had at home. See, it wasn't a lie. Just like another story she told. Recently, Kevin's mother had to go into the hospital to have a knee replacement. Unfortunately for her, there were complications, and she had to remain in the hospital for a few days without a knee while the infection went away. "Dad, Grandma is going to die." *"No, she's not."* "Dad, you can't live without a knee." *"Yes, you can, Caroline."* "No, you can't. My friend's grandmother had to go to the hospital and they took out her knee and she died right then." *"Which friend? I'll just call over there and find out if that really happened."* (Pause to reload.) "OK, Dad. I was just thinking, it didn't happen." *"Then why did you say that?"* "To prove a point, Dad." *"What point?"* "THAT YOU DIE WITHOUT A KNEE, DAD. DUH." *"So, let me get this straight. You made up a story to prove a point that's false?"** Caroline wagged her head and then thrust her finger into Kevin's gut, a Half Ellen, flawlessly executed. Kevin shook his head. *Why on earth*, he wondered, *would anyone make up a lie to support a premise that's not based in reality?* Then, at that very moment, the realization dropped onto Kevin's head like an anvil on concrete, or like something equally heavy onto something equally hard. That's exactly what *he* does for a living. Kevin felt very conflicted for a long, long time. Upset at Caroline, yet quite proud of her. And 2001 was the year Ellen turned forty. Kevin told her he remembered when he was in junior high and his English teacher, a woman they all called Old Lady Potts, turned forty. Kevin is now married to Old Lady Potts. That kind of grossed him out, because she has to be in her midseventies by now. In May, Kevin went to the pet store for cat food and came home with a black Lab. Something to feed the cat. Something to eat the cat. Nice trade-off any way you look at it. He named the dog Jay, after a friend at work. His name is Jay, too. Finally, Kevin had a male he could bond with. Kevin and Jay take long walks, talk about baseball, scratch themselves, and poop on the sidewalk together. One moonlit August night, while taking their evening stroll and talking about girls, Jay opened up to Kevin. *"You know something, Kev?"* "What's that, Jay?" *"I noticed something about all the females at obedience school."* "What's that, Jay?" *"They're all a bunch of bitches."* "I hear you, pal, I hear you."** In November, the Suttons got their second new pet of the year. A parakeet. His name is Flip. So now the cat spends its days staring at the bird, licking its chops. The dog spends its days staring at the cat, licking its chops. Ellen spends her days looking at Kevin, wondering why. Katie is five and in kindergarten. Julie and Kelly are twelve and in seventh grade. Beth is fifteen, in tenth grade, and starting to drive. Ironically, her sisters are starting to drive her nuts. A few weeks ago, she was driving her dad and her sisters to dinner, when the following scenario occurred. Caroline was in the back seat singing a song at the top of her lungs (probably not the Billy Joel song, "Honesty"). Meanwhile, Katie was shouting out in excitement as loudly as she could every time she saw a Volkswagen Beetle, a limo, a dog, anything with a horse on it, vegetation, the color magenta, cheese, or any carbon-based life form. On top of all that, Julie and Kelly were in the back of the minivan practicing for their school's Full Contact Debate Team. That day's topic was "The Death Penalty, Is It Ever Justified?" Kelly took the affirmative, with a well-crafted, brilliantly executed argument: "If you go into my room one more time, Julie, I'm going to kill you." Julie's counterpoint, while terse, was equally brilliant: "Oh, yeah?"* After twenty minutes of full-scale rioting by her four sisters, Beth had finally had enough. She turned to her dad and said, "God, they're annoying." Beth, unlike Caroline, speaks the truth.

Merry Christmas and Happy 2002. From Kevin, Ellen, Beth, Julie, Kelly, Caroline, and Katie. Aka, the Suttons.

*Actual conversation.
**Not actual conversation.

2002

Brother, can you spare $100,000?

Last week Kevin woke up with a nagging feeling. And being married to Ellen for nineteen and a half years, he has become an expert on nagging feelings. (Even though it's nineteen and a half years, Kevin happily notes that it feels like no more than eighteen and a half years. Nineteen, tops.) This feeling, though, was worse than that nagging feeling he'd had a few months earlier when he came home from a friend's bachelor party without pants and couldn't for the life of him remember if he had on pants when he left for the party. (Ellen was fairly adamant it was yes. But according to Kevin, it's a hung jury, which is probably not the best choice of words.) No, this nagging feeling had a more familiar, more painful refrain. Olsen-Twins-movie-like painful. It was the feeling of impending financial doom. Five daughters and a wife will do that to a man. (Two daughters alone would probably do that, too, but that's sour grapes at this point. Which is probably not the best choice of words, because it was the sour grapes of Sutter Home white zinfandel that got Kevin into this mess in the first place.) But the perspiration dripping off Kevin's forehead that morning wasn't due only to the fact that Jay, the ninety-pound black Labrador retriever Son That Kevin Never Had, was lying on top of him with his noneating end precariously close to Kevin's face. No, this was the sweat of a man who just realized he was about to lose everything. "Oh my God," it finally (just then) occurred to Kevin and he bolted up in bed, "Beth is going to college in a year and a half." Ellen, realizing this had nothing to do with her platinum status at the Visa corporation, turned away and went back to sleep. So Kevin did what any self-respecting father would do when faced with the looming specter of paying for his child's college education. Flee the country. He slipped on his shoes, reached for his wallet, grabbed his keys, and drove off in his car. Except for the wallet part. And the car part. You see, there wasn't enough money in his wallet to buy a dot-com. Apparently during the night, Beth, with loving concern not to awaken her weary dad, sneaked into Kevin's wallet and took out the sixty dollars she badly needed for a new towel and swimsuit for diving. And Kelly, with loving concern not to awaken her weary dad, sneaked in and took out the twenty dollars she badly needed for cheerleading pom-poms. (She couldn't buy just one pom for ten dollars; she had to have two because "everyone else had two.") Julie, with loving concern not to awaken her weary dad, sneaked out twenty dollars on principle alone. ("If Kelly gets to steal twenty dollars, so do I.") Katie, with loving concern not to awaken her weary dad, sneaked out three dollars to buy a candy bar from a Boy Scout who was selling them door-to-door for two dollars. All this taking from Dad's wallet really disappointed Ellen. After all, there was clearly a ten-dollar bill that the girls had overlooked in Dad's wallet, which was a cause of grave concern for Ellen. Is she not raising her girls right? If they haven't already mastered the basics of an elementary-level course like Dad as ATM, could they possibly be ready to move onto advanced debt-inducing classes? Like, Surprise, I Went to the Mall with Your Visa Card: A Practical Application. Or the masters-level program, Cajones in a Vise through Home Mortgage: How to Beat a Man into Submission in Thirty Short Years. Ellen, it seems, has her work cut out for her. Only Caroline, dear sweet honest-as-a-day-is-dark Caroline, was respectful enough not to sneak into her dad's wallet while he slept. She was quick to point out, however, that the five-dollar bill she had in her hands did not come from Dad's wallet, no it didn't, and if someone said it did then they were lying liars, and besides, nobody could prove it, Your Honor, unless they were in the room or they were videotaping it, and she was pretty sure nobody was videotaping it, so she would repeat it once again, loudly, THE FIVE-DOLLAR BILL SHE HAD IN HER HANDS WAS HERS AND IT DIDN'T COME OUT OF DAD'S

WALLET. Even if Kevin's wallet hadn't been fleeced like an altar boy in Boston, there was the matter of the getaway car. He no longer had one. Beth had taken that when she turned sixteen and got her driver's license in June. It was classic Ellen "What's Yours Is Mine" teaching. Kevin had always prided himself on keen financial planning. What follows are his nine simple rules for accumulating wealth (originally he had ten, but one of them wasn't that funny): 1) Don't play poker on payday. 2) Don't go grocery shopping on an empty stomach. 3) Don't bring your wallet to church. 4) Don't bet on a horse named Tripod. 5) Don't take a credit card to a "gentleman's club." 6) Don't pay for cable when you can steal it from your neighbor (if our neighbor is reading this, it's not yours, it's our other neighbor's). 7) Don't tell your wife you went to a "gentleman's club" (this will cost you half your assets in most states). 8) Don't tell your family you have a job (this will cost you all your assets in every state). 9) Enron. So, with no money and no car, nowhere to go and nothing to do, Kevin resigned himself to simply going downstairs and reading the paper. His name wasn't in the obituaries. Good thing. Ellen's "Desperate in Dallas" letter hadn't yet made it to Dear Abby. Good thing. So he turned to the horoscope section: "Cancer, June 21 to July 20. Don't marry, then decide to have a child and have a daughter, then decide in two and a half years to have another child and have twin daughters, then wait five years and have a fourth daughter, then wait eighteen months and have a fifth daughter. That is a recipe for financial disaster." Those horoscopes are always so vague. So here Kevin and Ellen are at the end of 2002 (as well as at the end of their rope). Beth is sixteen, a junior in high school, and has taken up diving. Hopefully her sense of direction with diving (jump straight down and look for water) is better than with driving. A few months ago, Beth got lost going somewhere in the car. She called Ellen on the cell phone for directions. Ellen asked her, "What direction are you heading in now?" *"Forward."* Julie and Kelly are thirteen and in eighth grade. Julie has a way of cutting straight to the heart of the matter. One day she was complaining that Kevin didn't give her enough money to go to the mall, so Kevin responded with the legally obligatory, "Julie, I'm not made of money, you know." Without missing a beat, Julie replied, "Yeah, you're made of fat, and too bad the bank doesn't take that or we'd be rich." Kelly wants to be an actress, and Kevin is always encouraging her to practice her craft. "Just act like I gave you money for the movies." Why she doesn't find that funny is beyond Kevin. Caroline is eight and in third grade. She came up with the most ironclad defense of the year. One day, Katie came downstairs crying, with Caroline innocently tagging along behind her. (This actually happened 362 days in 2002, but for our purposes, let's just focus on this one particular day.) Kevin asked Katie what had happened. She said Caroline hit her. *"Is that true, Caroline?"* Kevin asked. "Yeah, but I didn't hit her for a reason." Oh, then, sorry, the state apologizes and you are free to go, Mr. Bundy. Six-year-old Katie is in first grade. On November 30, 2002, she uttered the words that completed Ellen's Circle of Daughterhood: "I want everything. Is that too much to ask?" So now, here we are in the season of giving and sharing, and all Kevin and Ellen ask is that you find it in your heart to give, and send us a check for a hundred thousand dollars. For expenses. And pom-poms. Is that too much to ask? Ellen thinks it's a knee-jerk reaction on Kevin's part to panic now about college tuition. And, having been married to Kevin for nineteen and a half years, she's an expert on jerks.

Merry Christmas from Kevin, Ellen, Beth, Julie, Kelly, Caroline, and Katie Sutton.

2003

Miracle surgery.

In early October 2003, a neurosurgeon in Dallas made international news and gained instant worldwide fame when he successfully separated two conjoined Egyptian twins, Mohammed and (what was the other one's name? It might have been Carl or something). It was a much-celebrated thirty-six-hour surgery that the medical community heralded as a medical miracle. The insurance community just said, "Ouch." The doctor who performed the miracle surgery became an overnight media celebrity, appearing on the international talk-show circuit, including, *It's a New Day, Dallas; Good Morning, America;* and *Better Caves and Gardens, Egypt.* Meanwhile, just blocks from the Dallas hospital that made Mohammed and Carl's surgeon famous, another surgeon, Kevin Sutton, doctor of Hold It Down, I'm Trying to Watch a Baseball Game in Here, toiled in relative obscurity while performing the exact same miracle procedure nearly 250 times in 2003 on the Sutton twins, Julie and Kelly. Whereas the Egyptian twins, Mohammed and Carl, were attached at the head at birth, the Sutton twins, Julie and Kelly, were born attached to each other's throats. In a series of meticulous, touch-and-go surgeries performed over an excruciating twelve-month period beginning in January, Kevin (with the aid of his lovely assistant, Ellen) navigated that delicate balance between life and death—successfully separating clumps of Julie's hair from Kelly's clenched fists, removing Julie's boot from Kelly's butt on a number of occasions, as well as repairing the crippling effects of she-looked-at-me-itis and the all-too-tragic affliction commonly known in simple layman's terms as get-out-of-my-room-atoid. The following is a list of the things Julie and Kelly fought about in 2003, in no particular order and by no means complete: 1) Bras. 2) Underwear. 3) Socks. 4) Driving. 5) Parmesan cheese. 6) The Human Genome Project. 7) Lint. 8) Lithium and the entire family of -ium compounds, including but not limited to actinium, americium, berkelium (or what Julie calls ber*ju*lium), and cerium. 9) Whether the cat smiled. 10) Who stinks worse. 11) Hair and hair-related products such as shampoo, conditioner, and brushes. 12) Laundry. 13) The Internet and the computer. 14) The television and the remote. 15) The Professor and Mary Ann. 16) Military air space over France. 17) Pronouns and their proper antecedents. 18) The number eighteen. 19) No, it was the number seventeen. 20) No, it wasn't, it was eighteen. 21) You're stupid, it was the number seventeen. 22) You're ugly, it was the number eighteen. 23) Cereal. 24) Duct tape. 25) Unimportant stuff. Whereas the surgeon who operated on the Egyptian twins, Mohammed and Carl, can be pretty certain the procedure took (in other words, their heads aren't going to grow back together), sadly, that is not the case with the Sutton twins, Julie and Kelly. Theirs is a recurring condition that they will, to the unfortunate dismay of everyone within a ten-mile radius, have to wrestle with (ironic choice of words) the rest of their lives. As you probably know by now, unless you were, like, on *Apollo One* and you just caught the return flight home (in that case, welcome back; you're not going to like what happened to the Jackson Five, especially that cute little one, Michael), Julie and Kelly are just two of the five children that made the Sutton household a haven of warmth and cheer in 2003. Beth, who is seventeen and a senior in high school, has had to wrestle with serious medical conditions of her own this year. Kevin and Ellen began noticing that she was having real difficulty with her vision, unable to make out certain shapes and objects. When asked to clean the family room floor, for instance, they noticed that Beth would often find it hard, if not impossible, to differentiate a simple wadded-up towel on the floor from the actual planks of wood that make up the flooring surface. Sadly, she would leave the towel lying on the floor while looking directly at it, seeing a clean room. In fact, things the average non-vision-impaired person would take for granted, such as detecting a simple pair of socks draped over the arm of the couch, or making out an object such as an empty glass that was on a coffee table, Beth's brain simply cannot process. With time and therapy, Kevin and Ellen are confident, however, that Beth can one day regain the normal sense of cognitive sight that others enjoy. Kevin and Ellen's other two children, Katie and Caroline, seem healthy. Or at least, seem to display a healthy rivalry toward each other. Caroline is nine and in fourth grade. Katie is seven and in second grade. Oil is to water as cats are to dogs as Britney is to clothing as Caroline is to Katie. They share a bedroom. Bad idea. A "let's start a chain of Michael Jackson day-care centers" kinda bad idea. A "hey, I know, let's let the pet dingo sleep in the nursery with the baby" kinda bad idea. They like to pick on each other. One day Katie was trying to help Caroline decide what to give up for Lent. "It has to be something that's a huge sacrifice, Caroline," Katie eagerly pointed out. "How about if you give up lying?" And so that is how Caroline gave up lying for Lent. True story. Lately Katie has had trouble with talking in class. Last week, while Katie was telling a long story at the dinner table, Caroline, in a sincere effort to help her little sister not get in trouble in school, pointed out: "You need to be quieter in class, Katie. Why don't you practice at home? Like right now." It's touching just knowing that Caroline cares enough to help her younger sister get through these challenging times. Caroline authored a few more noteworthy quotes in 2003. Here is a list, in no particular order: 1) "I didn't hit Katie, I only hit her back." 2) "I can't get to sleep, my brain's too full." 3) "This is the reason not many people like you, Dad." 4) "My room's not messy. It's organized clutter." 5) "Moms don't respect their people." 6) "I'll tell you one thing, when I grow up I won't have a dad like you." 7) "Why do you only pay attention to me when I say stuff you don't want to hear?" 8) "I don't like this dinner because I don't like dinners that stink." 9) "I don't like you, Dad. I never have, really." 10) "I don't want everything in the world. Just one of everything." So, as 2003 winds down and the Sutton girls do their best to separate Kevin and Ellen from their sanity, Kevin and Ellen would like to take what might be their last coherent chance to leave you with their wish for the holidays: here's hoping you find the same joy in your lives that we've been so fortunate to find in ours. Sorry.

Merry Christmas and Happy 2004 from the Suttons. Kevin, Ellen, Beth, Julie, Kelly, Caroline, and Katie.

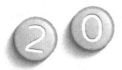

THE VASECTOMY STORY

After I found out Ellen was pregnant for a fourth time with our fifth daughter, I decided to take matters into my own hands. Had I done that a few months prior, maybe she wouldn't have been in this predicament.

I decided to get spayed or neutered.

At my initial consultation, my vasectomist, the oddly named Dr. Sever, gave me the speech about this being forever, which I thought was strange because I see billboards all over town for vasectomy reversals.

He gave me a pamphlet that stated I was strongly encouraged to shave my ball sack, which I did not do. I am not from Brazil, I am not gay, nor am I a porn star. I do not shave my ball sack.

I don't recall too much about the actual day of the surgery, just that Ellen dropped me off, happily. The day they render you as infertile as Kirk Cameron's career is really a woman's proudest day.

I do remember, as the nurse was shaving my ball sack, I apologized to her for not doing it myself, and asked if I should tip her. No is the answer to that one.

The next thing I vaguely recall was being in Dr. Sever's office with Ellen. He was giving me—well actually giving *her*, since my mind was in Saturday-night-Lohan mode—the postsurgical consultation.

Dr. Sever told me to make sure I "cleaned the pipes at least a dozen times before attempting sex."

"If you tell my wife it's a hundred times," I apparently said, "there's an extra thousand dollars in it for you."

Two of the three of us thought that was amusing.

Honestly, I'm pretty proud that I was able to come up with something so insultingly funny under the most trying of circumstances. But Karma repaid me, as Karma often does, and as my children rarely do.

One other piece of postsurgical advice Dr. Sever gave me was to go home, lie down, put a bag of frozen peas on my crotch, and relax. Don't do anything to aggravate the situation, and take it easy for a few days.

I guess, after seeing what he saw down there, he didn't suggest frozen carrots on account of not wanting me to be intimidated.

Kelly was the first to see me. It was a Friday, and she had just gotten home from school. School was six houses down from us, so the kids walked home and sort of came in as they came in, and Kelly was the first to come in and discover that Dad was home early on a Friday.

She raced home that particular Friday because this was her Special Friday.

Every Friday I designated as a night I would spend with one of my daughters. We went in order: Beth, Julie, Kelly, and Caroline. We would see a movie, get ice cream, race go-carts, bowl, go to the indoor rock-climbing place, whatever. Each girl got to pick. Which explains why I saw the Spice Girls movie three

Fridays in a row. And why Special Friday sort of lost its luster not long after that.

The girls looked forward to Special Friday. But this particular Friday wasn't so special for an important part of me. I was zoned out on my bed, the TV on, the frozen peas strategically in place. (On a side note, that day I watched a scene from a *Perry Mason* episode that perhaps more than anything dramatized how much public sentiment on drinking and driving has shifted between the early 1960s and now. A drunk client of Perry Mason was escorted back to his car and told to "drive it off" in the cool mountain air.)

Kelly had hit the jackpot. Dad was home early, her special day was about to begin. She ran to the bed and jumped on me, landing right on my lap. I have taken a fastball at full speed into my nuts. At that very moment, I was dreaming of that very moment.

I rolled out of bed, onto the floor, and writhed in pain as Kelly went on and on and on about going to this new place that lets you make tile mosaics and you get to glue things and then paint them and that was what we were going to do for her Special Friday.

Kelly dashed out of the room to go get ready for the tile place. I envied the broken tile.

I heard the front door open. The parade was home from school. Ellen told them, "Girls, Daddy is home from work early today, but he is not feeling well, so let's not bother him, and no matter what, do not jump on him today."

She didn't get the chance to pass along that key piece of information to Kelly.

One by one, I heard the girls run up the stairs, stand by my door, see me hunched over on the floor, and run off to play. Yep, Mommy didn't lie. Daddy's home. OK, enough of him. Barbie time.

Ellen came upstairs and immediately scolded me. "Why are you on the floor? You are *not* supposed to be out of bed. And why is that bag of peas over there? If you don't do what Dr. Sever instructed, you will never heal."

She slammed the bedroom door. It took me about seven minutes to crawl the eight feet from where I was on the floor to the door. I hit the lock. I passed out right there to the sound of Kelly banging on the door and repeating, "Daddy, I'm ready. Daddy, I'm ready. Daddy, I'm ready. Daddy, I'm ready. Daddy, I'm ready. Daddy, I'm ready. Daddy, I'm ready. Daddy, I'm ready. Daddy, I'm ready. Daddy, I'm ready. Daddy, I'm ready. Daddy, I'm ready. Daddy..."

Two days later I got a call from a friend. Rudely, I had forgotten that it was Sunday, the day of the finals in our flag football league, and we were going for the championship. If I didn't show, we'd have to forfeit. Having recent man-altering surgery was not a valid excuse.

I begged off, telling him no way could I play flag football that day. But he was looking out for my well-being. He reminded me that I needed fresh air, and that it was noncontact—all I had to do was hike the ball and stand there. He was thoughtful enough to point out to me that what I would do was no different than picking up the remote to change channels, which was what I had been doing the last three days.

That sounded logical.

It was a chilly Sunday in January by Dallas standards, about thirty degrees. I took my pain medicine, made my way to the field, and spent four ten-minute quarters casually hiking a ball and standing there as a flag football game unfolded around me.

Then I went home and slept. Honestly, to this day I do not remember anything about that game, except we didn't have to forfeit because of me.

Seven days later, I was about to discover the number-one side effect of postvasectomy flag football.

Pittsburg, Kansas, is about as far away from anything as any one thing could be from any other thing, equidistant as Beth is to a cookbook. That turned out to be a huge problem—because that was where I was shooting a video for an educational services company.

The first day of our shoot went well. Day two, not so well. I woke up and something wasn't right, like going to a movie and realizing they cast Jennifer Lopez in the role of a character you're supposed to take seriously.

As the morning went on, it worsened. Every ten minutes, a pain that seemed to be emanating from my gut grew sharper. I thought I must be having appendicitis or something. By noon, I couldn't stand straight.

The closest hospital was in Joplin, Missouri, about forty-five minutes away. And, when you got there, you'd be in Joplin, Missouri. Kansas City was about two hours away.

They dropped me off at my hotel around noon, when I couldn't take the pain any longer. By the time I got up to my room, I was sweating and felt like I was going to pass out. I thought the best thing might be a shower and then to sleep off whatever I had.

It was then that I discovered what I had. A right testicle as large as a grapefruit.

Every time I breathed, it was as if an evil elf was kicking me in the right nut with his little evil pointed elf shoe. And as the day went on, his evil elf shoe grew sharper and the grapefruit grew larger.

For those unaware, a right nut the size of a grapefruit is not normal. I needed to get some help. Soon. I got on the phone and called around. There are no swollen testicle experts in Pittsburg, Kansas. Keep that in mind if you must travel there. Bring your own.

Renting a car was out of the question. There are no rental car places in Pittsburg, Kansas, either, although the local Chevy dealer would let me use a car to drive around town for a spell if I wanted. I guess you never know when you have an urge to parade your elephantine testicle around to the good people of Pittsburg, Kansas.

I had to get to the hospital in Kansas City. I was informed that the guys in the film crew's lighting truck were planning to take the lights back to Kansas City—but not for four more hours. That was my best bet. So I watched TV to pass the time. I think it was *The Elephant Man*.

A lighting truck, I discovered, has really crappy shocks, and doesn't go much faster than fifty miles an hour.

It was three and a half hours of having my right nut snapped with a wet towel. Thwack, thwack, thwack, thwack, thwack, thwack, thwack, thwack, thwack, thwack, thwack, thwack.

They dropped me off at a hospital in Kansas City around seven thirty. I was rushed right into the ER. That's what they do with Grapefruit Testicle.

Apparently, I caught a virus while playing flag football that attacked the weakest part of my body. Which, because of my vasectomy, was in my nut sack.

For the record, because I asked, shaving it myself would not have mattered.

The needle the doctor used was about six inches long. After that I don't remember much. I remember screaming. I remember getting a prescription for a pain reliever with codeine. I remember seeing an evil elf scamper away. I remember checking into a hotel across the street.

Fourteen hours later I woke up. My right nut was no longer a grapefruit.

I crawled out of bed, looked in the mirror, and said to myself, "Sex did this to me."

MY DAY IN COURT

There's a reason the most popular profession in America is being a lawyer. From the minute they can talk, girls are the world's best defense attorneys.

You, as the father, are the hapless Hamilton Burger to their Perry Mason. You never stand a chance.

Did you not read the script?

INT. COURTROOM – DAY
Your daughter—for the sake of dramatization, let's call her CAROLINE—sits in the witness box, smugly acting as her own defense lawyer.

You, as the prosecuting attorney—and let's say we name this character KEVIN—pace back and forth, assessing the precise time to pounce. You decide that time is now.

KEVIN
And do you recall the last words I told you before I caught you painting the neighbor's car with cat poop in your new dress?

CAROLINE
Yes, I remember.

You stop pacing and stare at CAROLINE intently, waiting for her to illuminate on her answer.

It occurs to you that the only illumination in your house comes from every single damn light bulb in every single damn lamp in every single damn room being left on every single damn night by every single one of your damn daughters, causing every single one of your damn electric bills to come in at north of 450 damn dollars a month.

You wait for her to say something more, but, tapping into your vast courtroom experience, you remember that the only time a female does not talk is when you really want her to.

You stare at the witness.

KEVIN
And can you share with the court what I told you?

CAROLINE
I don't remember.

KEVIN
But you just told the court that you did, in fact, remember.

CAROLINE
(shifting nervously)
I did remember, but I just remembered I forgot.

KEVIN
Did I not tell you not to go out that door?

CAROLINE
Wait, are you asking me if you did not tell me not to go
out the door, or if you did tell me not to *not* go out the
door? Double negative question are so confusing. Do you
not not agree?

KEVIN
(angry)
Did I tell you *not* to go out that door?

She sits defiantly, refusing to answer. You look to the bench for
help.

The JUDGE—a rapidly aging woman who looks similar to the
woman you married a long, long time ago and who was quite
something back in her day, that exact day traceable to the day
before she first found out she was pregnant—refuses to intervene
due to conflict of interest. Plus, she was gone when this happened
and distinctly recalls telling you not to let the girls go outside and
ruin their new dresses, and puts the blame for this totally on your
shoulders. The JUDGE glares at you with her best testicle-
retracting glare.

JUDGE
I told you not to let them go outside.

Backed into a corner, you spring into action.

KEVIN
Did I tell you not to go out that door, Caroline?

CAROLINE
I didn't go out that door. I went out the window. The defense rests, Your Honor.

The JUDGE pounds the gavel. Case closed.

You stand there, stunned, defeated again, your record in court a pitiful zero wins to 4,692 losses. You are the Chicago Cubs of dads.

SMASH CUT TO: You imagine your dream day in court. It would end with the JUDGE declaring that the DNA tests proved they are not, in fact, your daughters, and you are owed the three million dollars in child-rearing fees you have already spent.

SMASH CUT BACK TO: That dream is short-lived, and you are reminded that the Chicago Cubs have another home game.

THE FATHERHOOD LOOPHOLE

If you're going to be a father, get yourself a bathroom.

I discovered early on that the only times I can ever get a moment of privacy from my girls are those rare occasions I selfishly go to the bathroom.

Once I lock that door, nobody bothers me.

(A saccharine sidebar: One day, when I was in the bathroom, three-year-old Katie knocked on the door. I told her I needed my privacy. She spent the next twenty minutes walking around the house, calling out, "Privacy. Privacy." She went looking for it for me. It has yet to be found.)

I realized I could get away with murder behind the locked bathroom door. Ellen and I had never discussed a set time limit for how long she would allow me to use the bathroom. So I decided to stretch those moments of privacy and shrill-free living to ninety minutes at a time.

Once she realizes she hasn't badgered me in the past seventeen minutes, she will instinctively call out, "Kevin."

I always have a free one that I don't need to respond to. I explain later that I didn't hear her.

The second one, she makes sure I hear.

"KEVIN, WHERE ARE YOU?"

"I'm in the bathroom."

This is the only legitimate reason for me not to immediately drop everything I am doing and run to her side the very second she calls for me.

No matter what I am doing, it is not as important as what she needs done, which is usually very unimportant.

She called out to me one day, "Kevin."

I didn't respond. I was kind of busy.

"KEVIN!"

"I'm on the operating table."

"I'm back from the grocery store."

"I'm having open heart surgery."

"I've got groceries that need to be brought in."

"My chest has been cut open and my internal organs are exposed."

"YOU BETTER NOT LET THAT MILK SPOIL."

That's why I love the bathroom. In there, I have a free pass. I can do the crossword puzzle. Eat some powdered doughnuts. Watch a baseball game. Pound down a few beers. Learn a vocation. Once, I took a crap.

It's my time and I take as much of it as I can.

Ellen is convinced I have a life-threatening intestinal disease. I can live with that.

WEDDING BLISS

Men love golf. Women love weddings.

Women drive from church to church on Saturday mornings looking for weddings to attend. They watch wedding dress shows on TV. They wistfully read stories about far-off royal weddings and hope someday their Prince Charming will sweep them off their feet.

Then reality sets in. Guys like me come along.

So when we were invited to a wedding in Austin one year and had to RSVP, the vote was six to one in favor of going. It went to committee.

I argued on behalf of the negative voters, reasoning that the lawn had not been cut in nearly six days, and there was a huge concern that the two beers in the garage refrigerator would pass their expiration date and would have to be thrown out.

A decision was rendered. We would attend the wedding.

It's not that I didn't want to spend a weekend away with my lovely wife and our five charming daughters. It's just that there is absolutely nothing more dreadful than transporting six females and all their female crap.

I have estimated, and this is not a joke, that roughly 23 percent of my life is wasted waiting. Waiting for one of them to use the bathroom so we could leave. Waiting for one of them to find a hair thing so we could leave. Waiting for one of them to dislodge the kitchen knife from the other's back so we could leave.

The wedding was Saturday evening. We needed to leave around noon on Saturday to make it in time. To prevent us from being late, I announced to everyone that we were leaving Friday night at eight. That gave us roughly a fourteen-hour margin of error. Experience had taught me that we'd need it.

After dinner that Friday night, I packed and was ready to go in four minutes. What slowed me down was the fact that it took me three minutes to both discover someone had broken the CD player by inserting ten poker chips into the drive mechanism, and to ferret out who did it.

Experience taught me to look at Caroline. Experience taught Caroline to pass the blame onto Katie. She whispered to her little sister, "Katie, look at Daddy and say, 'I did it.'"

As if a string had been pulled on the back of a doll, Katie said, "I did it."

Caroline pointed her thumb at Katie, shrugged her shoulders, and gave me a "what are we gonna do about the little one?" look. I put the 150 dollars for a new CD player on Caroline's tab and went to the car to wait.

It was five minutes to eight on Friday evening. I waited and I waited.

On Saturday, at about 12:55 p.m., I started noticing signs of life. Screams of agony and betrayal were coming from somewhere upstairs. Doors were being slammed in faces. Curse words were being flung. The Sutton girls were preparing for another road trip. Already more than fifty-five minutes late. Right on time.

So now we had to hurry. I never have to worry about getting a speeding ticket because I am fortunate to have six radar detectors.

We got near Austin and then had the arduous task of figuring out where our hotel was. It was, somehow, my fault that we forgot to bring the piece of paper with the hotel address on it. I suggested driving back home to get it, but it was pointed out to me that if we did that, we'd miss the wedding altogether. I hadn't thought of that.

We knew we were staying at a Hyatt; we just weren't sure which one.

Taking a chance, I pulled into the Hyatt up ahead. I told Ellen I'd run in quickly and ask the guy at the desk if we had reservations there.

Beth came with me. Beth was always the one with the common sense to get out when she could.

She and I went to the front desk. Of course, there was a line. Being in a hurry always has a line.

Finally, it was my turn. Just as the front desk guy asked if he could help me, and just as I was about to speak, I was interrupted by the voice of a crazy woman.

"Excuse me. My key doesn't work."

She wasn't talking to me, so I didn't pay it much attention. The front desk guy was politely doing his job helping the next person in line, who happened to be me, so he didn't pay attention either.

That didn't sit well with the crazy woman.

"I SAID, EXCUSE ME, BUT WE GOT UP TO OUR ROOM AND OUR KEY IS NOT WORKING AND I DEMAND A NEW KEY THAT WORKS RIGHT NOW!"

I turned to look at her. She was in a bridal gown. Her new poor sap of a husband was next to her, doubling as her shadow. Married all of maybe two hours, he was already a beaten man. His shoulders were slumped and he gave me the universal "sorry about her, dude" guy nod.

I thought this was a good time to teach Beth a lesson about the rudeness of others.

So I said to the lady, "Sorry, but I have a car full of girls out there and all I want to do is find out if we have reservations here. It will just take a second."

She looked at me as if she was Oprah and I was a diet. "I DON'T GIVE A DAMN ABOUT YOUR CAR FULL OF KIDS, THIS IS MY WEDDING DAY AND THIS DAMN HOTEL SCREWED UP AND I CAN'T GET INTO MY ROOM."

As the front desk guy quickly recoded her key, I locked eyes with the new groom. I felt so very sorry for this kid.

I looked at him in pity and said sadly, "This is the rest of your life, man. The rest of your life."

His till-death-do-us-partner snatched the card from the front desk guy and then barked at me, "Screw you, asshole." She stormed away, dragging her sad sack of a husband along.

I discovered this was, indeed, our hotel. I went to the car and told Ellen and the girls to pile out; we didn't have much time to get ready.

As we were making our way through the lobby, Beth looked at Ellen and said, "Dad made a bride lady cry."

Ellen thought to herself, *That's not the first time.*

PUBLIC ASSISTANCE

Eventually, when you have daughters, the discussion turns to allowance.

Kids expect to be paid simply for the act of being kids. We are raising the next generation of welfare recipients.

They don't bring in a dime of income, yet they expect everything for free: food, rent, clothing, cable, water, Internet, candy, iTunes, toys, heat, electricity, maid service, flat walls on which to draw graffiti. No wonder kids don't have a care in the world. They don't have a bill in the world.

The best one to give money to was Kelly. She just liked holding it. She would earn a dollar for cleaning the bathroom, and clutch that thing like it was Amanda Bynes hanging on to her career.

I'd give her a dollar at noon, and at seven that night she would be in her nightgown perched in front of the TV with that coveted dollar bill still tightly squeezed in her hand. Then, inevitably, she'd fall asleep. I would put her in her bed and take the dollar out of her hand.

The next day, she'd wake up and forget about the dollar. And we'd do it all over again.

She would earn that exact same dollar bill about a thousand times. Thank you for the lessons in thievery, Mr. Bank of America.

When my girls lost a tooth, they would find all sorts of fun stuff under their pillows: assorted coins, a paper clip, a poker chip, maybe a guitar pick, a key to something, a feather, a bottle cap, maybe a pocketknife or a film canister, dice or a rock. The morning after the Tooth Fairy came was really fun.

I was cleaning out my closet recently when I ran across a folded-up piece of paper I had forgotten about. It was a contract that the twins had entered into with Katie back in 2001. It was in Julie's punctuation-challenged chicken scratch:

> "This note says that when Katie is 15 she will give Julie $50 dollars because Julie (her favorite sister) was Kellys maid on September 30 2001. (10 years from now.) This note proves it so Katie, give me <u>50 dollars</u>. Kelly owns me (Julie Sutton) 9 dollars when she is 15 also."

Underneath they signed their names:

Katie = payer

Julie Sutton = getter

Kelly Sutton = maid/eyewitness

Where were they planning to get this money in ten years? Earn it? That's a good one.

Nope, they were going to be part of the largest redistribution of wealth in human history. It would come from the family financial kingpin they call Dad.

2004

Stupid dog.

Greetings, gentle readers:

In a much-welcome break from tradition, this year's Sutton Family Christmas Letter will be written not by the dull, dimwitted one that the short, shrill ones call Dad. Rather, it will be scribed by me. My name is Jay. Perchance I have sniffed you before. I am the Suttons' black Lab. (We prefer the term Labrador American.) Not a day goes by that one of the short, shrill ones, more commonly known as the Sutton kids, fails to call me a stupid dog for one thing or another. "Stupid dog, you ate my toast." "Stupid dog, you're sitting on my shoe." "Stupid dog, you incorrectly conjugated that verb and made me flunk Spanish." "Stupid dog, you missed your exit." It's always stupid dog *this* or stupid dog *that*. Perhaps they didn't realize that while they were busy filling their minds with the brilliance of *Desperate Housewives* and MTV's *Punk'd* (ah, the classics), I was pursuing my dream of Shakespearian writing. Or maybe I was just licking myself. Who can tell the difference? In any event, after reading this letter about the events that unfolded the past twelve months, you be the judge of who is the stupid one. So, here I go. There have been many famous years throughout history: 1492, The Year Columbus Discovered America; 1776, The Year the Declaration of Independence Was Signed; 1813, The Year Right After the War of 1812. Around here 2004 will forever have its name etched in the collective conscience as what Katie, the youngest of The

Shrills, coined "The Year Everything Broke." Why? Because it was the year that everything broke. The string of misfortune began in February, when Kevin lost his job. Bam, just like that, no more avocado lavender dip flea baths for yours truly. Back to licking myself clean. Do you have any idea where a dog's mouth has been? I do. March and April seemed to go by pretty smoothly. May, though, saw a return after a too-brief hiatus of a Sutton Girls' original: *Naked Girl Boxing*. But with a whole new cast. This season, Caroline and Katie were in the roles first played by Julie and Kelly. Daily episodes explored the trials and tribulations of five girls growing up in a house with just four showers, and the inevitable coming-of-age lesson such harsh sacrifices teach. In one particularly memorable episode, as Caroline left the shower, she executed a perfectly timed half hissy fit reverse back kick on an entering Katie. In a surprise twist ending, it was revealed that Caroline did, indeed, kick Katie for a reason. It seems Katie had heckled her for the entire duration of the seven seconds she had to wait for Caroline to come out of the shower. Subsequent episodes of *Naked Girl Boxing* featured the ever-popular "You Took My Shampoo and I Need It Now" (with the award-nominated fight scenes, in high-definition Shrillvision for increased realism), as well as the always-pleasing "You Used My Towel So Now I Will Be Forced to Slap You." In a touching nod to tradition, Julie and Kelly made cameo appearances in Episode Six as the antagonists. June is when things got really bad. One day, when my usual session of romping and pooping in the backyard had run its course, I wanted to come back inside (hey, I was hungry, and the hole in the fence wasn't big enough for me to escape— believe you me, I have tried). Well, it seems that holding the door open for all of the three seconds it takes me to get inside was just too daunting of a task for these girls to perform. So, impatiently, they slammed the back door on my tail before I was all the way inside, whacking off about an inch. There I was, standing in the living room, my newly severed tail whirling around like a bloody propeller, spewing blood all over the walls, all over the floor, all over the ceiling, all over everything in its path, and what did I hear? "Stupid dog, you're getting blood all over the place." Pardon me, but have your tail whacked off and see if you turn into Martha Stewart. Stupid humans. To top it off, I had to suffer the humiliation of walking around the neighborhood for six weeks with the tip of my tail wrapped in a dorky white bandage, the canine equivalent of the Kick Me sign. I was ostracized from the Butt-Sniffing Club. Things got really out of control later in the month. With Ellen and Beth out of town on a college orientation trip and Kevin at work, one of the four remaining Einsteins failed the demanding Flush the Toilet test. Somehow, they let the toilet overflow. And overflow. And overflow. And, in accordance with the laws of plumbing and gravity, that overflowing water had to flow somewhere. One guess where it went. On me. There I was, casually enjoying a rare moment's quiet, when all of a sudden, the sky fell. Or, to be more precise, about a hundred pounds of wet Sheetrock fell. On me. The entire ceiling in three rooms came crashing to the ground, water ruining the floor, walls, and electronics. There I lay in a weird mixture of wet Sheetrock, water, sewage, wires, and plumbing, and I thought to myself: Hey, wait a second. When I want to poop, I go outside, and one of those humans picks it up and disposes of it, outside. But when they, on the other paw, want to poop, they go *inside* (inside, where they live, mind you), where they have developed a complicated and elaborate plumbing system just to carry the waste back *outside* to some remote (and I can only imagine godforsaken) place far, far away. Perhaps a Taco Bell. Once again, I ask you to decide: Poop outside, let a human pick it up for you. Poop inside, cause twenty-two thousand dollars' worth of damage to your home and property. Stupid humans. The brilliance continued in July. Beth, while leaving a deserted mall parking lot after work one Sunday evening, somehow managed to drive an almost brand-new VW Beetle into a light pole. Not one of those elusive, dancing light poles you read so much about. No, this was a just-standing-there-not-moving light pole. You know the kind. Big cement base with a pole sticking out, stretching high up in the sky and a light hanging off the end. You can't miss them. Unless you're Beth. It took nineteen thousand dollars and two months to repair. Stupid humans. In August, Beth conveniently went away to college at Auburn. (If you're reading this, Beth, one word of warning: last time they sent me away, I came back without testicles. Beware.) Soon afterward, the family took a trip to Florida. Just in time for hurricane season. Nice move, brainiacs. They came home to find their stereo had been stolen. Apparently, the guys who were putting in the new floor to replace the one damaged as a result of

a failure to master the intricacies of flushing, left the garage door open one afternoon. "Hello, burglars, welcome to the Sutton House. Make yourself at home. See anything you like, take it home with you." Then, as a final and cruel reminder that The Year Everything Broke isn't over quite yet, just five days ago Ellen got hit in the eye by one of Caroline's fastballs. The ball hit her square in the eyebrow. There she was, standing in the middle of the softball complex, her newly ruptured eyebrow spewing like a bloody volcano, shooting blood all over her, all over her clothes, all over the softball field, and all over everything in her path. And does she hear, "Stupid Ellen, you're getting blood all over the place"? No, of course not. She fainted. But that's beside the point. She wouldn't have heard it anyway because nobody says things like that to humans. Instead of verbal insults, they whisked Ellen away to a hospital for three stitches on her eyebrow. Now her eye looks like she went to an NBA game. Of course, while at the hospital, Katie conveniently lost the key to Ellen's car. Kevin, by the way, was out of town. So here we are, in mid-December, looking back at the year that wouldn't end. A broken tail, a broken house, a broken car, a broken face, a broken-into house. As I bid farewell to this, The Year Everything Broke, I leave you with one thing. My fondest wishes for a Merry Christmas and a break-free 2005. Well, actually, I leave you with two things. Go look on the living room rug. Stupid humans.
Sincerely,
Jay, the dog

The preceding letter was not endorsed by Kevin, Ellen, Beth, Julie, Kelly, Caroline, or Katie Sutton. Except for that part about having a Merry Christmas and a Happy 2005. Oh, and Kevin thought that "testicle" joke was a lot funnier than Ellen did, who finds things like that highly inappropriate for a Christmas letter. But what can you do? The dog wrote it. Stupid dog.

2005
PART ONE

December 10, 2005
Dear Midol:

My name is Kevin Sutton. I have a wife and five daughters. You make a PMS pill. We need to talk.

Are you aware that there are four weeks to a month? Then, can you explain to me why on this sweet Earth your beloved and necessary product is designed for only one week?

What were you thinking? Because of this unfortunate and inexcusable oversight, your product benefits mankind only 25 percent of the time. (And by that, I do mean *man*kind.) A 25 percent productivity rate is, quite frankly, shameful. Imagine if the garbage man picked up only once a month. Imagine if Starbucks was on only one corner of every intersection. Imagine if Aristotle's fourfold causality theory was, laughably, simply a onefold causality theory. I mean, that's just crazy talk.

You get my point? Of course you do. Get your scientists working on those other three weeks. And please get back to me by next Thursday on that. Please. By next Thursday. I implore you.

Oh, another thing: according to the bottle's label—and believe me, I have studied that thing closer than the media have studied whatever it is that's going on over there in that Iraq place—your product is designed to relieve cramps, bloating, fatigue, and swollen breasts. That's it? That's the best you could do? (And I got to tell you, frankly, that swollen breasts thing's not a problem as far as I'm concerned.) Pitiful. Just pitiful.

Perhaps if the guys in R&D over there at Bayer Pharmaceuticals were actually guys, your product would relieve all those other equally prevalent recurring monthly female symptoms as well, such things as: Anxiety. Headaches. The feeling of impending doom often accompanying late-night poker games. Prickly heat. Questions, questions, and more questions. Eye Rolling, Stages One through Seventy-Four. Spontaneous verbalization (especially prevalent during playoff and World Series time). Feelings of adequacy. Lack of short-term memory. Eye Rolling, Stages One through Seventy-Four. That really annoying feeling of never being wrong. That feeling of wanting to jump out of her skin and, of course, the associated act of landing under mine. Loss of libido. Stewing. Scrapbooking. Emotional roller coastering, and the entire emotional amusement park, including seven dollars for parking. Irritable bowel syndrome. Grouchy bowel syndrome. Oh, Come On, Now You're Being Totally Unreasonable bowel syndrome. Uncontrollable use of the word *disappointment*. Scurvy. Sudden loss of emotional control. Sudden loss of ironing skills. Sudden loss of motor skills, especially while motoring. Shingles.

And let's be totally honest here: your Midol Teen Formula just doesn't work at all. Not one bit.

Otherwise, explain to me the rationale for paying one hundred sixty bucks for a pair of jeans, as my sixteen-year-old daughter Kelly did. Heck, you could buy two eighty-dollar pairs of jeans for that money. Or explain to me the rationale behind leaving your twin sister stranded and crying at school because you absolutely couldn't wait an extra six seconds for her to come out, as my other sixteen-year-old daughter Julie did a few weeks ago. Explain to me that four-hundred-dollar text-messaging bill my nineteen-year-old daughter Beth racked up last month at Auburn University. UR KLN ME.

And don't even get me started on what I have to look forward to. Both my eleven-year-old daughter Caroline and her antagonistic nine-year-old sister Katie were recently diagnosed as HIT Positive. Yes, they have full-blown Hissy-fit-In-Training, along with associated hissy fit-like symptoms such as hissy twitch, hissy stomp, and pre- and posthissy bitch slap. Just last week Caroline asked me if she could have another little sister. I informed her that her mother and I were finished having children (see "Loss of Libido" above). She replied, "No, a different one than Katie."

While I'm at it, let me tell you about another situation where your company's product recently failed. In October, Indians took Ellen's job. No, not the same Indians who took two hundred dollars from me at the blackjack tables this past April. Not American Indians, 7-Eleven Indians. Her job was shipped to Bangalore, India, very, very thanks come again. My God, you should have heard the crying I had to put up with. One suggestion: a Midol Outsource Strength Formula would come in very handy from time to time. She can't even look at a Big Gulp anymore without breaking down.

Believe me, I've conducted a twenty-two-year focus group and would gladly share my findings with you, many of which might shock you. One or two might actually make you say, "Dagnabbit."

Now, before you run off and accuse me of being some incredibly handsome, athletically built, almost-god-like-in-physical-features chauvinist, I know it's not right to judge an entire group of people simply based on the actions of 99 percent of them. For instance, the common stereotype that all fast-food workers are Mexican is not true. In reality, many of them are Mexican American.

I know it's a cliché to say that women are overly emotional. But "dogs can't play violin" is also a cliché, and how many beagles do you see in the symphony? Hey, how else do you explain *Moulin Rouge*, *The Sisterhood of the Traveling Pants*, the Lifetime Network, Fabio, Tom Cruise jumping on Oprah's couch, Oprah, Ricky Martin, unscented Secret, or the entire therapy profession?

I could go on and on, but I have to wrap this up. I just remembered I told my wife Ellen that I'd write the family Christmas letter about all the joyous and wonderful times we had in 2005, and wish everyone a safe and healthy 2006 from everyone in our family. Instead, I ended up writing this. God, I'm sure I'll never hear the end of that.

Come on, Midol 24/7/365. Come on.

Yours in saving hu*man*ity (wink, wink),

Kevin Sutton

2005
PART TWO

December 15, 2005
Dear Midol:

My name is Ellen Sutton. Recently my stupid husband sent you a letter. As always, I would like to offer my deepest apologies for anything he may have said or implied that could have in any way been offensive to anyone at your company.

I would like to begin by apologizing to all the women who may have taken offense to his caveman-era views on gender. As your scientists have probably alerted you to, their brains are very, very small.

Apologies go out to the wonderful people who have given their lives creating Midol. I just love your product. Period.

I apologize to garbage men, Starbucks (although I must say four dollars for a cup of coffee borders on gouging), Aristotle, Aristotle's heirs, and Aristotle's estate.

A big sorry goes out to the news media. After all, I am forever indebted to you for your thoughtful and in-depth coverage of important issues such as Jennifer and Brad, Britney and Kevin, Nick and Jessica, Tom and Katie, and the entire Hollywood scene. Hey, if those other places like Iraq and the Middle East were so great, why do people spend so much of their time blowing them up? If Hollywood taught us anything, it's why declare war when it's so much easier to just dump someone?

I would like to apologize to Indians, both Native American and those from the country of India. Even though you took my job, there are no hard feelings. I still love your ink.

Another apology goes out to Mexicans and Mexican Americans. It is totally understandable that one could confuse "large *fries*" with "large *Sprite*."

I would like to apologize to my children. (After all, I have spent so long apologizing *for* them, it's only fair.)

Sincere apologies go out to violinists, Oprah, the producers of *Moulin Rouge* and *The Sisterhood of the Traveling Pants*, the Lifetime Network and its respective cable outlets, Ricky Martin, the psychology profession, and Secret deodorant. Frankly, though, I am with him on that Tom Cruise thing. What a wussy.

Well, I think that covers it for now.

Again, please accept my deepest and sincerest apologies for any insensitivities in my husband's letter to you. He was supposed to write the family Christmas letter where he wishes all our friends and family a wonderful Christmas and a safe and prosperous New Year.

But, like our stupid dog, he has an attention span of about five seconds. Also, like our stupid dog, he has been neutered.

Yours in sisterhood,
Ellen Sutton

P.S. You guys aren't the ones who make Viagra, are you? If so, I have a bone to pick with you.

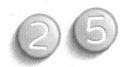

THIS HAPPENED

"Hey, Ellen, I'm going to the store to pick up some deodorant. Do you need anything?"

"Oh, I'm glad you reminded me," she said, glad that I reminded her. "Since I'm having that procedure on Monday, I can't have any food after three o'clock today. Can you pick me up a box of clear-colored popsicles?"

On the list of the top one thousand things I would have ever guessed she'd have asked for, clear-colored popsicles were no higher than number 1,873.

Trying to figure out what the hell she was talking about, I asked her, "A box of clear-colored popsicles? What the hell are you talking about?"

To clarify, I was not wondering why she seemed so certain that clear-colored popsicles came in boxes, but rather that they came at all.

"You know, popsicles that are clear. I can't have anything with color or anything."

"Who sells clear popsicles? Isn't that what ice is? Have you ever, in your entire life, heard of or seen clear popsicles in any store in any city or town or municipality, in any state or province or commonwealth, in any nation or republic or occupied territory in which you have ever been? I mean, they color popsicles for a reason. They make popsicles purple so they taste like grape. Red popsicles are cherry. Orange popsicles are, surprisingly, orange flavored. What flavor would clear be?"

She actually seemed to be agitated by this question. "I don't know. Maybe lemon."

"Wouldn't those be yellow?" I'm sorry, but that is a perfectly valid question.

"I don't know. What about, like, diet lemon?"

"Diet lemon popsicles? Wouldn't those be discontinued for lack of sales?"

"Just see if they have clear ones," she said as she walked off.

I came home with a box of tampons. Honestly, I really wasn't sure what else to do in that situation.

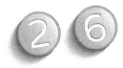

THE RACE TALK

Perhaps no single topic in America ignites more passion and divides more people than race.

The subject is one of the more difficult discussions to have with your children, yet one of the single most fundamentally important legacies you will pass along.

They say kids are like sponges. (I've found them to be more like bank-draining sinkholes, but for the time being, let's go with the sponge analogy.) Your kids see how you interact with others. They learn from you. Not just from what you say, but from what you do, especially when you are at home, away from society's eggshell, where the "real you" comes out. (There, and in karaoke bars.)

I am a product of 1959, and we dealt with race issues much differently than today's generation.

But even today, after everything this country has been through, it seems nobody can talk about the race issue comfortably. Even if you have the most liberal views on the subject, you still cannot broach the topic of race in a social setting without a cautious whisper, without looking around the room to see who is within earshot, and without measuring your words more carefully than TGI Friday's measures its liquor pour, which is a reference to something that is carefully measured, lest they give you more than you paid for.

Honestly, and I am not proud of this, but from the time I can first remember breathing, I can remember it being bred in me to hate the other race. Where I come from in Indiana, we were openly hostile toward the other race, and everyone who sympathized with it.

Today, in polite circles, they say, "the N-word," but in my generation we called a spade a spade.

We called it NASCAR.

We hated stock car racing and everything surrounding it. I am from Indianapolis, home of the Indy 500. Sorry if it sounds racist, but the Indianapolis 500 is the superior race.

So when Kelly informed me that she wanted to go to a NASCAR race with her high school friends, I put my foot down.

No daughter of mine was going to sympathize with the enemy in the War Against Southern Aggression.

EVERYTHING IS MY FAULT

Having a wife and five daughters means that, at any given moment, anything you do will piss off anywhere from one to six people.

Usually six.

So all you can do is make the decision you think is right and move on.

Mostly, your logic and reason and common sense are not met with understanding and acceptance and rationality. Mostly, they are met with blame and disappointment and scorn.

I was at work one afternoon. It was a Monday after a weekend spent painting the living room. It was summer, so all five young daughters were home. Admittedly, not the easiest situation for Ellen to deal with while trying to work.

I get a frantic call from her. Apparently, the girls had just ruined everything and it was all my fault.

Blame, disappointment, and scorn on line one.

"OK, what is going on?" I reluctantly asked.

"Your daughters went into the garage."

"The daughters I had from my previous marriage?"

"What? You were married to someone before me? You have other kids? What are you talking about?"

She didn't realize how preposterous what she had just said was. The idea that once one had a set of daughters from one wife, one would voluntarily have a completely other set of daughters from another wife, was just foolish.

I calmly explained, "You said, '*your* daughters,' meaning they were *my* daughters and not *our* daughters. I just assumed some daughters of mine that you didn't know about must have shown up."

"Don't be an a-hole, Kevin. The girls got in the garage and got into the paint and got it all over them."

I waited for the point of this conversation. It wasn't coming.

"I'm sorry to hear that, but why are you telling me this?"

"You put the paint in the garage."

"Where else was I supposed to put it?" I figured putting it in the Barbie room would have been wrong. "I put it in the garage to keep it out of reach of the girls."

"Well, it obviously didn't work. They got into it."

There was an underlying "you stupid penis-addled male screwed up again" tone to the tone of her voice. I didn't particularly care for that.

"Uh, OK. Let me get this straight. The girls have two parents, you and me. Right? One of us is at home, one of us is ten miles away at work. Right? Which means, one of us is ten miles away from the door leading into the garage, and one of us is right there to prevent the girls from going through that door, which I am ten miles away from, and getting into the garage and playing in the paint, which I am ten miles away from. Right?"

Silence.

I took that silence to mean, "Once again, you are so right and your wisdom is so sage, Kevin, what was I thinking?"

Sagely, I hung up the phone and went back to work. So I could afford more paint.

THIS EXPLAINS EVERYTHING

They say opposites attract and, in my case, this couldn't be truer.

Ellen is a decent person. She has the integrity of an oak tree. Her moral compass points due north. She rarely swears, she dislikes promiscuity, she is a wonderful mother, she'd probably be the last person on Earth to download porn. Am I making myself clear? She is a decent person.

So I was totally shocked to hear her talking like a drunken sailor on shore leave one night.

All seven of us were in the living room, winding down from a day of being our family. Ellen was relaxing in a chair reading John Irving's *The Cider House Rules*.

Not Norman Rockwell, but also not Norman Bates. Until Ellen ran across a word in the book that piqued her interest. She said it out loud.

"Jism."

The word just hung there. I had no intention of touching it.

She had no intention of letting it go. She proceeded to read out loud from the book: "'When he heard the water rushing through Three Mile Falls, he would remember the songs that pumped like jism…'"

Then she looked at me and said, "That's a fun word." And to show me how fun it was, she said it again, like she was learning it off a foreign language record, "Jism."

Caroline looked up and said innocently, "Jism, Mommy, jism gism." She went back to her puzzle. Beth went back to Katie. Julie and Kelly went back to coloring. Ellen went back to reading. I wanted to go back to that day before I met Ellen, but I couldn't.

All I could do was announce, "OK, girls, time for bed." I had to get them out of that room before Ellen started quoting from *Lady Chatterley's Lover*. We could pronounce all sorts of fun words like orgasm and Pap smear and such. I had no idea what the hell was going to come out of her next.

I put the girls to bed and came back downstairs. Ellen was still reading.

"What the hell was that all about?" I asked.

"What do you mean?"

"Why on Earth did you shout out the word jism in front of the girls?"

"I thought it was a funny-sounding word."

"So are vaginal discharge and Penis McScrotum, but you don't hear me blurting out those."

She looked at me blankly. She had no idea what I was talking about.

"You mean to tell me you don't know what the word jism means?"

"No. I never heard it before."

"Oh, come on, Ellen. Everybody knows that word."

She didn't. I told her, and she was shocked. Shocked that she had said that in front of her daughters, for sure. But more shocked that I insisted it was a common word any woman would know. She was convinced I was wrong. So she told me to call a friend and see if his wife had ever heard the word.

That was a weird phone call.

"Hey, Wade, I got a question to ask you. Can I talk to Diana and ask her if she knows what jism is?"

"Of course she knows," was Wade's natural guy-response. It's almost as if you are questioning a man's manhood asking something like that. Even so, he put her on the phone to help in my social experiment. It turns out she had never heard that word before. He and I were both surprised by that.

I called another friend. I got the same "of course she knows" response from him, and the same "nope, never heard that word before" from her.

I called a third friend, and a fourth friend. Same thing. I started wondering, *Are we, like, in the twilight zone or something?*

Ellen reasoned that maybe it's because guys were just disgusting pigs and women had a little class.

That did it. I called my friend David. His wife is from New Orleans.

She knew.

2006

Greetings from moist Khanti-Damor.

It is with heavy hearts that the 2006 Sutton Family Christmas Letter® comes to you this holiday season. After twelve wonderful years in Dallas, Texas, the Suttons said good-bye to our many good friends and neighbors (and that damn dog on the next street over that won't stop barking at all hours of the night) and left behind a life of leisure and relatively lesion-free living to embark on the next chapter of our lives. Howdy! (Or should we now say Jhaudii?) This letter comes to you from our new home in the tiny village of Khanti-Damor in the remote Jhabua District of Western India. Initially we came to India searching for the job Ellen lost to these good people in the fall of 2005. What we found instead—past the Slim Jim aisle and the prepaid phone card display—was the ideal place to call home. Sure, it's a village with deplorable living conditions; one with no running water, no medical care, no Internet poker; one with brutal heat, brutal savagery, Brut for Men. Sure, on the surface, life in Khanti-Damor seems extremely harsh, almost unbearable. Cannibalism, for instance, is openly practiced (here it is called *khénébél*, which translates literally into English as "Hot Pockets"). The murder rate is the highest in the world (two more murders, though, and you're in the running, O. J., so come on, find that killer in you!). The average temperature is 145 degrees Fahrenheit (but it's a moist heat). The village is in the stifling grip of its twenty-fifth consecutive year of severe drought (think Kevin Federline's career, divide by two). And the village's local professional baseball team, the Khanti-Damor Cubs, really, really sucks (there's nothing to add here, but since the last four sentences ended with something in parenthesis, we didn't want this one to feel left out and start a run-on epidemic). But while it has been labeled the "Most Miserable Place on Earth"—having recently edged out the Afghan-Iraqi border, Branson, Missouri, and the BCS headquarters—Khanti-Damor is not without its positive features. On the bright side, life expectancy is the lowest in the world. Pillaging is down 6 percent. Lepers are no longer allowed to "gimme five." Hurricane season is over (but then there are the playoffs). Mating with oxen has been outlawed by nearly every tribe. And most importantly, and the root of why we moved deep in this land that time forgot, the tribes of Khanti-Damor practice the most progressive of customs: the sacred law of *bhangjad*, otherwise known as "reverse dowry." It is a simple yet brilliant practice that dictates interested men must pay a hefty sum of money to the bride's father in order to marry his daughters—even more if she is educated (dagnabbit!). It is this spirit of the progressive bhangjad that lured Kevin Sutton, social pioneer, to relocate his family to what would otherwise be the underbelly of civilization: the lawless, the corrupt, the unwashed, the Hillary in 2008 supporters. (Editor's note: The Indian government is trying to put an end to the practice of bhangjad, calling it unfair and inhumane. This is the same government that, hypocritically, has no problem charging a buck seventy-five for a Big Gulp. To register your support for bhangjad with the Indian authorities, call any US company's toll-free hotline and ask to speak to customer service. The prime minister will be with you momentarily, very, very thanks much you.) So, in a show of solidarity for our new tribesneighbors of Khanti-Damor, the following is Kevin's published price list for each of his daughter's bhangjads:

ITEM/ASSETS	BHANGJAD
BETH, Age 20	
32 teeth, all straight	2½ million American
2 ears, one a bit droopy	dollars or a PlayStation 3
2½ years college math	
JULIE, Age 17	
Fastball, underhanded	2,000 hens, red
Curveball, underhanded	100 yaks, black
Dropball, underhanded	50 cows, brown
Compliments, backhanded	1 greatest hits of Barry, White
KELLY, Age 17	
2 pierced ears	$600,000 or a son to be
1 pierced bellybutton	named later
0 licks of sense	
CAROLINE, Age 12	
	$5 – no returns, all sales
	final
KATIE, Age 10	
4,282 stuffed horses	1 glue factory
183 books on horses	
27 framed pictures of horses	
82 horse-riding lessons	

SPECIAL LIMITED-TIME OFFER: In the event of his sudden and most untimely death (perhaps caused by this very paragraph you are reading), Kevin is taking prepaid orders on Ellen. Anyone having 2007 Texas Rangers season tickets behind home plate, she's yours. Respond soon.

Well, time to slaughter the mongoose for the annual Feast of Punjab the Obstinate parade. So in conclus— (Editor's note: Ellen just read the preceding paragraph. Consequently, this letter has come to a sudden and most untimely end. You are, however, reminded to have a Merry Christmas and a great 2007. And, to make an offer. No reasonable one will be refused.)

The Sutton Family Christmas Letter® is a registered trademark of Sutton Family Worldwide and its seven subsidiaries.

Christmas® is a registered trademark of the United States Shopping Mall Consortium.

Family® is a registered trademark of the Conservative Christian Coalition.

2007

Sutton family, party of four.

After eighteen long, brutal, grueling, painful, shrill, costly, stressful, loud, distressing, gut-wrenching, sticky, disquieting, scabby, difficult, unpleasant, weepy, emotionally trying, accusatory, caustic, bloody, money-draining, overly dramatic, fleshy, hair-pulling, girl-kicking, car-wrecking, gaseous, deceitful, estrogen-fueled, irrational, moist, argumentative, nauseous, mostly deafening, and, apparently, jacketless years, Julie and Kelly have left home for college. Finally. Julie at Indiana University, Kelly at Texas State. Hopefully, four and a half states' worth of separation will be enough to keep them from kicking and biting and pulling out each other's hair. Time will tell if geography can solve what genetics and parenting could not. Kevin is reminded of a talk he had with them earlier this year after one particularly meaningless fight (it was preseason and did not count in the rankings). He sat them down and reminded them that they are twins. "I have two of you," he said. "I really need only one. One of you is spare parts." This was another year in which Kevin failed to receive a coveted World's Best Dad mug. So, as 2007 ends, and with Beth, Julie, and Kelly out of the house, the Sutton family has gone from a party of seven to a party of four: Kevin, Ellen, Caroline, and Katie. From zone defense to man-to-man. Kevin often wonders why they call it a "party" of four. Aren't parties supposed to be fun? For instance, listen to how festive the following party sounds: "Hey, come over for cake and ice cream and some ring toss, and we're going to play Kick the Can." That's a normal party. That's a fun party. Now, compare it to the party raging daily at the Sutton House in Dallas, Texas: "Hey, come over for door slamming and screaming and some accusation flinging, and we're going to play Kick You in the Crotch." Unfortunately for Kevin and Ellen, it's a party they have to RSVP to. Caroline is now thirteen and femaling at a level that makes even women say, "Wow, that's annoying." Recently, after suffering through the intense physical and mental trauma associated with being asked to undertake her annual room cleaning, and narrowly surviving the near-death experience of bending over to pick up things, Caroline, after four hours of cleaning, declared in plain three-hundred-decibel English, "YOU CAN STOP YELLING AT ME NOW, PEOPLE, MY ROOM IS CLEAN." Yet, clean is the only thing that could not be found on her floor. The following is a partial list of what was, indeed, found: 1) Eight hundred nineteen dollars in assorted coins, bills, jewelry, silverware, and meat. 2) Sixteen drinking glasses, four broken. 3) Seven cereal bowls, three broken. 4) Twelve promises to clean her room, all broken. 5) Seven dinner plates filled with half-eaten snacks in various stages of decay. 6) Twenty-three new strains of fungi. 7) Eight hundred twenty-two pairs of socks, sixty-four pairs of underwear, and twenty-two paramecia. 8) Six hundred thirty-one Scuncis, hair attached. 9) A throbbing gooey unrecognizable substance, hair attached. 10) An assortment of unmentionable feminine protection products (note to the makers of Always: your fine "napkins" have proven to be insufficient at sopping up throbbing gooey unrecognizable floor substances). 11) Box cutters (hmmm, come to think of it, where was Caroline on September 11?). 12) Gum and gum-related trash. 13) Fast food and fast-food-related trash. 14) Candy and candy-related trash. 15) White trash (a Britney Spears CD cover). Caroline is in eighth grade and mostly devotes her time to dance, all forms—ballet, tap, modern, jazz, and dancing around the truth. Every day is a surprise party with Caroline. The kind where you walk in the door, people yell, "Surprise!" and you collapse with a heart attack. Hurray! The party rages on with Katie, who is eleven, in sixth grade, and is showing amazing skills at lack of reason and a sister symptom of PMS that is commonly known as SIUTRYHOAFITAMTISASILYS (Sudden Irrational Urge to Rip Your Head Off and Feed It to a Mongoose Then Instantly Smiling and Saying I Love You Syndrome). Kevin has come up with a nickname for her: Li'l Lucifer. It's adorable yet frightening at the same time. Just like Katie. Katie has become the neighborhood terrorist. Ellen routinely takes her wrapping (what we growing up in Indiana used to call TPing), the act of wrapping some unsuspecting neighbor's trees, shrubs, and house with toilet paper, then laughing as they wake up the next day to see their house has been transformed into Full Mississippi. Ellen is currently teaching Katie how to hotwire cars and steal stereos. Julie is like the caterer to the party. She sets up things, leaves, and then sends you a bill for it all later. Julie called home to say her account at Indiana University was frozen and she was unable to register for her spring classes. Ellen was perplexed. An account? Frozen? How is that possible? What account? *"I don't know,"* Julie responded, *"they send me a statement every month. It says I have a balance of sixteen hundred dollars. Not sure what I'm going to spend it on, but it's frozen so I can't get to it."* Ellen was curious. "A balance? What are you talking about?" Julie answered, *"It says, 'balance due, sixteen hundred dollars.' And they keep adding to it every month."* "Uh, Julie," Ellen patiently explained, "balance due means it's what's due to *them*, not due to *you*. And that money they're adding to your balance, they call those late charges. Did you think they were paying you to go to college or something?" Ellen forgot to ask the important Dad-question. What the heck was she spending sixteen hundred dollars on? They had better do some serious colleging on that girl up there. Before Kelly left for college, she brought a heaping pot of stew-pidity to the party. One night she told Kevin, "Dad, I need a jacket for tomorrow." Now, at first blush, that's an innocent enough request. Many kids need many jackets for many tomorrows. Yet it is not a reasonable request when made at 1:30 a.m., which is when in fact that particular request was made. Kevin and Ellen were sound asleep when Kelly burst into their room and declared her dire need aloud, very aloud, "DAD, I NEED A JACKET FOR TOMORROW." While Ellen slept, Kevin told Kelly to kindly get the heck out of his room and go to bed. While Ellen slept, Kelly, assuming Kevin didn't hear her properly the first time, repeated, more loudly, "DAD, I NEED A JACKET FOR TOMORROW." While Ellen slept, and realizing that not one of the words coming out of Kelly's mouth were, "Sorry to bother you at one thirty in the morning and for waking you out of your deep sleep with a foolish request for you to instantly whip up a jacket out of thin air," Kevin suggested Kelly leave immediately. While Ellen slept, Kelly's mouth kept moving with more words that Kevin ignored because they were being spoken out loud. So, finally, Kevin relented. "OK, Kelly, go downstairs and look in the phone book for an all-night jacket store, and I'll take you right now." Kelly left. The next morning when Kevin came downstairs for breakfast, he found the Yellow Pages on the kitchen table, opened to the J's. She tried. You just can't find a decent all-night jacket store anymore. What did Beth bring to the party this year? Cat pee. You see, earlier this year, Beth moved in with new roommates who are allergic to cats, and unreceptive to cat pee. So Beth was gracious enough to ship her cat to us. Kevin is to cats as logic is to Caroline. Incompatible. Caroline is to logic as Beth's cat is to a litter box. Just can't seem to find it. You know the old saying, "There's more than one way to skin a cat"? So far Kevin has come up with thirty-seven. Technically, the "Machete Maneuver" and the "Columbian Eviscerator, Version Six" are similar, but still different enough to warrant their own inclusion. If only Michael Vick had chosen cats instead of dogs, he'd be in the Hall of Fame right now instead of in jail. Beth is graduating this month from Auburn with a degree in applied math. She has yet to find a job. Please, if you have any math that needs applying, call Beth. Please call soon, so she can take her cat with her. With or sans skin. Call soon and Kevin will throw in a pair of cat-fur gloves and matching cat-fur slippers, eyes attached. Fortunately, having a wife and five daughters has given Kevin thick skin. Lots of thick skin. Mostly congregating around the lower abdomen. As for Ellen, she is just happy to have a loving, caring, understanding, patient, wonderful, giving, attentive, Adonis-like, witty, intelligent, sophisticated, well-groomed, pleasant, non-foul-smelling, sharing, carefree, snuggling, always willing to listen to those interesting three-hour stories about what happened today at work, funny, sensitive husband like Kevin. So, as the Sutton party winds down into the final days of 2007, Kevin and Ellen just want to say please have a nice holiday. Please have a great New Year. Please, dear God, let college get here quickly for Caroline and Katie. And for Kelly's sake, please, somebody, please open an all-night jacket store.

Merry Christmas from Kevin, Ellen, Beth, Julie, Kelly, Caroline, and Katie "Li'l Lucifer" Sutton.

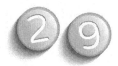

THROW LIKE A GIRL

Sports can be either the strongest bond a dad can have with his children, or the biggest wound he can inflict on them.

This is a topic that is very close to my heart.

Too many youth coaches are boorish, petty, arrogant egotists who project their misguided beliefs and failed sports glory onto the kids they coach.

Really, what does a six-year-old kid care about? Not winning. He cares about the chance to run around with his friends, the chance to put on a uniform and pretend he's Michael Jordan (or if it's a girl, LeBron James), the chance to go to the concession stand for candy and a drink.

Won-lost record, standings, stats, or the coach's lifetime arrogance percentage are things that don't mean a damn thing to a six-year-old.

For that age group, obsessing over wins and losses only brings out the Joe Paterno in people.

I remember a Saturday in Indianapolis during my first years of coaching Little League. I was walking away from the concession stand after a game when I heard, "Your team lost because of you. You weren't paying attention and you cost them the game."

I looked up and saw a dad, red-faced with anger, berating his son who was maybe seven. The kid was in tears. The dad even got angry that his son was crying. "If you're going to cry, you're never going to amount to anything."

I was in my early twenties and didn't have kids at the time. To this day I regret not having knocked out that jerk. I mean, the league issued aluminum bats to me for a reason.

Some of my fondest memories with my girls came from sports. If you're willing to keep it in perspective, it can be a wonderful experience for them, not just you. It's hard for many adults to keep it in perspective, though.

When I was growing up, I thought coaches were larger than life. They had whistles. But once I saw things through my kids playing junior high and high school sports, I realized that many coaches are teachers just trying to earn an extra few bucks coaching a sport they often have very little knowledge of.

Katie loved volleyball. She was on a team that traveled as far away as Atlanta to play in tournaments. She got so much joy out of playing. Until she got into high school and her ignorant coach asked her, in front of her entire team on the bus, "Are you retarded or something?"

Katie was crushed. Who does things like that? I was really proud that Katie wrote a letter at the end of the season telling that coach how awful she was, not just as a coach but also as a human being. Katie quit volleyball.

Thank you, dumbass coach. And dumbass human being.

Julie loved basketball, and was really good at it defensively. When she got to seventh grade, she made the basketball team. She was on cloud nine.

She didn't get to play much. Never, in fact. Game after game, we would go to the gym and watch Julie sit on the bench as her team lost game after game. They were not a strong team.

Finally, the coach noticed Julie existed. I saw her walk over and say something to her. I saw Julie shoot up off the bench and run to the scorer's table to check in.

She got in a game. She passed the ball in on an inbounds play, took a pass back, dribbled downcourt, and passed it off. Then her coach yanked her out of the game.

That was weird, I thought. Then I saw the coach approach Julie. She said something to Julie in front of all her teammates that made her cry and slump over.

What she said was, "Do you have any idea how many mistakes you made?"

How many mistakes could she possibly have made in the twelve whole seconds she was in the game? And who says that to a twelve-year-old kid? What possible motivation would any coach have for ripping a player to shreds, breaking her heart, and humiliating her in front of her peers?

I was furious. Ellen talked me out of killing the lady. I had anthrax delivered to her apartment, though, for good measure. But I didn't say anything to her because Julie asked me not to. She had to put up with this tree pig the rest of the season.

I held my tongue until after the final game of the season, another loss. The players and parents gathered at midcourt as the coach thanked everyone for a great season. She asked if we had any questions.

I had one.

"Coach, your team finished one and fifteen. Do you have any idea how many mistakes you made?"

I heard later that the coach was livid about being humiliated in front of her players and their parents, and she went into the locker room and cried.

It seemed like a fair question.

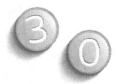

GOD LOVES A WINNER, GIRLS

Sports are a wonderful learning experience for kids. They teach them about teamwork, about success, about pride, about purpose. They even teach kids about God.

If your children are huge sports fans and make idols out of their favorite players, sports teach them that God's name is invoked daily as a cover-up for greed.

In the winter of 2012, the most-recent best hitter in the history of baseball, Albert Pujols, had a monumental decision. His contract was up and he could sign with any team. This was a man who had been with the St. Louis Cardinals his entire career. He was worshipped in St. Louis like a god.

Trouble was, the St. Louis Cardinals were not the American banking industry, pissing away money with no regard for common sense.

Pujols played for the Cardinals for ten years and made a fortune from that team. But now, at the end of the 2011 season, Albert's contract was up. He was a free agent. He could play anywhere he wanted.

Albert did some soul-searching. He told reporters that he would pray and let God make that decision for him.

And Albert did what any deeply Christian man would do in this situation. He hired an agent.

Apparently God didn't say to him, "Albert, go play for the Pittsburgh Pirates. They can't pay you much, but they have been horrible for twenty-five consecutive years and they sure could use you. You don't need the money, Albert. You've already made hundreds of millions of dollars playing baseball. Make a city happy. Be a baseball missionary."

Nope, God didn't say that to Albert.

And God didn't remind Albert to think of the crippled kids in Cleveland (many of whom play for that city's baseball team, the Indians), or the young fans in Kansas City who have spent their entire lives rooting for a crappy team owned by a Walmart heir, so they had no hope or reason to cheer (but they do get a coupon for a nine-gallon jug of pickles for just a buck ninety-nine!).

Albert asked God. And God apparently said what he always says in that situation, "Take the most money. Oh, and get the contract back-loaded. And get deferred cash. It's a huge tax incentive. The secret is the deferred cash."

So Albert signed with the Los Angeles Angels of Anaheim. A team with pockets so deep, it takes two California cities to fill them.

God always tells athletes to take the highest offer. I wonder why that is? Maybe he gets more in tithing.

My daughter Katie asked me once, "Why do the winning players always say, 'God was on our side.' Why does God want people to only win?"

I thought about this on a spring day in 2012 when I was in the stands at Rangers Ballpark and watched Josh Hamilton hit a game-winning home run in the bottom of the thirteenth inning to help the Texas Rangers come from behind and beat the Toronto Blue Jays.

Josh Hamilton had the flu. He was physically drained. In fact, in the fifth inning of that game, he got dizzy and almost passed out. But he stayed in. During a few at bats, he grounded out so weakly it looked like he was one of those crippled little Cleveland Indians that God forsook.

But somehow, with the game on the line, feverish, shaking, drained of energy, and sick, Josh Hamilton went to the plate and, with one mighty and improbable swing of the bat, found the strength to hit a towering home run to center field.

When he was asked after the game, Josh Hamilton informed everyone, "God was responsible for that."

I wondered what God had against Casey Janssen, the Toronto Blue Jays pitcher who threw that pitch to Hamilton.

Does God hate Casey Janssen? Does God hate anyone who grooves a fastball in the thirteenth inning? Does God hate Canada?

Did God hate the other team? Why? What did they do to him? Are losers godless as well as trophyless? Or is God from Dallas and, like all Dallas sports fans, he only loves a team when it wins and hates it when it loses? (If God is from Dallas, I wonder if my kids ever trick-or-treated at his house? I wonder if he gave out money. He seems to have a lot of it.)

Did God hate the fans of the losing team? Quite often those fans are from Cleveland. I've been to Cleveland, but I would never set the river on fire or let the city's team go more than sixty years without winning a World Series like Someone Who I Won't Mention Here has done.

Or, more likely, did God have money on the game? If so, that's got to be a clear violation of about a dozen gaming laws.

And why did God love the Rangers on the day Josh Hamilton hit that game-winning home run, and hate the Cardinals on the day that Albert Pujols signed to go play in Los Angeles of Anaheim, yet just a few short months before, God wanted those very same St. Louis Cardinals to beat those very same Texas Rangers in the World Series?

Pick a team, God. You're killing me.

Explaining to Caroline why God wanted her beloved Texas Rangers to lose the World Series was hard. It was equally hard explaining to Caroline why her beloved Texas Ranger hero, Josh Hamilton, said he was going to let God decide where he should go when he, too, was a free agent after the 2012 season, and, in a totally surprising move, he, too, left the Rangers for the team that offered him the most money.

Parenting is hard.

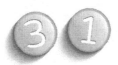

I USED TO BE CATHOLIC, BUT I GOT IT FIXED

Religion is something important to pass on to your kids. But for me, it was always a difficult thing to deal with.

I grew up Catholic, so most of my life was spent wondering why God hated me.

Moreover, I grew up Catholic in Indianapolis, Indiana, which right there is pretty convincing evidence that he at least mildly detests me. Growing up Catholic means you have the guilt of original sin thrust upon you the instant you were born. You start out batting zero for one, already on God's shit list.

Catholicism is like an asshole big brother. The minute you walk through the door you get blamed for crap you didn't do.

My parents were Catholic. My father was born in Lima, Peru, where everyone is Catholic, and went to Notre Dame, where the best Catholics get invited to attend. My mother came from Lithuanian immigrants who were Catholic. I had no choice but to fly the Catholic flag.

My parents sent me to Catholic school from the very beginning, and I was dutifully enrolled until a few weeks before the end of fifth grade, when the nuns at St. Luke's Catholic

School requested that I no longer attend St. Luke's Catholic School anymore.

From the earliest I can remember, I went to church seven days a week. That's a lot of dogma to inflict on a kid at such a young age. (Unfortunately, I never used the excuse, "My dogma ate my homework." I just thought of that one five minutes ago.)

Every Monday through Friday at school, our first class was Mass. We would religiously trudge to the sanctuary for a half an hour of Catechism class. We were supposed to use that time to pray, but they never said what we were supposed to be praying about. I mean, when you're seven, what could you possibly be passionate enough about to bother God for? I could barely form a bowel movement, let alone a cohesive message to the Man Above.

But, like the good soldier, I went to church every Monday through Friday and I acted like I was praying. Mostly I closed my eyes and hoped somebody would set that mean teacher of mine, Sister Charles Marie, on fire. She was a mean, mean nun who liked hitting me with rulers.

Yet I figured out early on that my prayers weren't being answered. Every time I opened my eyes, Sister Charles Marie had not been set on fire. Either nobody was listening to my prayers, or Sister Charles Marie's prayers of not being set on fire were trumping mine.

Why did God hate me? Why was this woman not on fire?

Around the time I hit seventh grade, I decided I'd start praying for something that would really make this a better world—seeing women's breasts. If something was going to come from all this, I figured it might as well be something attached to a nipple.

It was a long, long time before God answered my women's breasts prayer. Frankly, if truth be told, I think it was answered more by Boone's Farm strawberry wine than by God.

Every Saturday before basketball or football or baseball games, we went to church, too, to pray. Father Fry, who was our coach in every sport, instructed us to ask God if he could see a way for us to "beat the stuffing" out of our opponents, especially our archrival, St. Monica's. I remember once asking Father Fry, "But aren't the kids at St. Monica's praying to the same God to beat the stuffing out of us? Whose stuffing does God love more?"

He instructed Sister Charles Marie to hit me with a yardstick. Not being on fire, she dutifully obliged.

For the record, it seemed God mostly loved the stuffing of the teams from the other parochial schools in the Indianapolis area more than he did St. Luke's brand stuffing.

Of course, even though we went to church every day at school and every Saturday before athletics, we went every Sunday. Sunday is the moneymaker in the Catholic Church.

But the hypocrisy of my father about religion shaped me in a very profound way. All that religion my dad was paying good money to have pounded into our heads, all those Sunday mornings he whipped us with a belt for balking at going to church, all that was fine for us, but apparently it was something he didn't need.

He got all the religion he needed, apparently, from watching Notre Dame football on Saturdays. I can't remember my dad ever kneeling there next to me on those unpadded pews. Not once.

My mom and sisters went to the early service. That meant my older brother and I were on our own for the late service.

Every Sunday, he and I got dressed in our church suits, slipped on our church shoes, clipped on our church ties, and headed for church. Where we would walk in, grab a church program from the stack nearest the door, fold it up and put it into our church suit pocket, and then flee from religious persecution to go play and blow up things.

Later on, when my mom was hanging up our suits, she'd find the folded-up program, smile at how wonderful her churchgoing boys were, and nobody was the wiser.

My wife Ellen had a much saner religious upbringing. She was raised Methodist. Their team is SMU. (Ignore for this discussion that they once cheated so badly in football, they got the death penalty.)

So when we had kids, religion was something she felt strongly about passing on to our daughters. It was such a positive influence on her childhood.

I appreciated the moral compass religion instilled in them, so I was more than fine with our girls getting a strong religious upbringing. Frankly, I didn't care that it wasn't what I grew up with. So I switched over to her brand.

Even though I had used up all the coupons in my church book long ago, I went for my girls. Being a father means doing things for your children that are important to their spiritual upbringing. And if I was going to ask them to go, I needed to go myself.

Beside, Methodist pastors don't rape kids. That's a big selling point.

2008

Our stupidest year.

"School is stupid, homework is stupid, learning is stupid, Katie is the stupidest sister, we are the stupidest family, this is our stupidest year." Thus, in one long, grammatically challenged run-on sentence, Caroline Sutton smartly summed up her feelings for life, the universe, and everything else in 2008. But mostly her feelings for Katie. So, as we look back on the year, we ask: was 2008 really our stupidest year ever? Perhaps (Sarah Palin). Maybe (Thomas Beatie, the Oregon "man" who got pregnant who turned out to be a woman who got pregnant who turned into a man; thus, once and for all answering the question, where is Jerry Springer going to find his next generation of guests?). Could be (see the Paris Hilton movie, *The Hottie & The Nottie*). Probably (Ellen's idea to take the dog with us on our trip to Indiana). But one thing is certain, 2008 was surely a most historic year. On November 4, 2008, history was made when, in polling places across America, Barack Obama became only the forty-fourth man born to a white mother ever to be elected president in the history of the United States of America. Thus becoming our nation's first Halfrican American president. It wasn't just a victory for men born from white mothers. It was a victory for all people born from white mothers. Men, women, and everyone in between—like Thomas Beatie. Starbucks was so moved by patriotism, they offered everyone a free cup of coffee just for voting. The most popular order, according to Starbucks marketing data? Black, with cream. Oprah was so proud, she gained 365 pounds, one for every electoral vote Obama won. The election proved that not only does Oprah tell Americans what to read, what to watch, what to eat, what to drink, what to wear, what to think, and who to date, now she tells us who to vote for. But in encouraging news, in a recent survey Americans were quoted as saying they vowed to start thinking for themselves, as soon as Oprah tells them how. Also, 2008 was the year Kevin and Ellen Sutton celebrated twenty-five years of marriage. Why has Ellen kept Kevin around for twenty-five years? Maybe to prove that Caroline was right. Kevin has a way of saying things that get taken way out of context. He would, for instance, like to apologize to the dancers who performed the chorus line thing in skimpy outfits at a recent office function whom he stupidly mistook for strippers. Even though they came with more clothing than they ended up with, they were not, in fact, strippers. (At least, not very good ones in Kevin's book.) But, after twenty-five years, you'd think Kevin would wise up and be used to what happened just this very weekend. He was jarred out of bed by the pleasant sound of Ellen's "morning voice" with this: "Kevin, our house was wrapped last night. Get out there and clean up the toilet paper in the front yard." Now, usually Kevin is quite accustomed to dealing with toilet paper first thing in the morning. But normally it's a nice private moment, in the backyard. So he dragged himself out into the chilly December morning, climbed a tree, and started picking out toilet paper. Then he wondered, *Hey, wait a second, why am I stupid enough to be out here all alone at the top of a leafless, lifeless pecan tree in the middle of a chilly, gray December picking wet, soggy toilet paper off a bare, indifferent tree branch? Why isn't Ellen out here with me?* Then he remembered. Because Ellen possesses the female parts he so desperately covets. So while Ellen kept her female parts warm inside, a shivering, freezing, and decidedly much stupider Kevin—with suddenly smaller male parts—unwrapped the trees that the neighborhood thugs had so thoughtfully decorated. Kevin would like to point out, at the risk of making his wife look bad, that Ellen did indeed help. For instance, at one point she opened the door and, in her best helpful voice, said, "Kevin, do you need a ladder?" *"Yes, dear,"* Kevin replied, with a gentle lilt in his voice. (This might have been just a low, monkey-like grunt; he was too high up to properly hear.) "There's one in the garage," she so helpfully added before slamming the door. Tight. And locking it. And dead bolting it. And chain linking it. "Hmmm," Kevin said to himself, "a ladder in the garage? Who knew that's where ladders were—" *We interrupt this Sutton Family® Christmas™ Letter^SM to bring you this special news bulletin. The latest Middle Eastern cease-fire was shattered earlier today as Palestinian forces stormed the holy land of Israel's bedroom looking for the Sacred Straightening Iron. Hours of intense, bloody-murder screaming broke out all along the west bank of Israel's room as Palestinian rebels scoured the treacherous Israeli floor line looking for any traces of the Sacred Straightener and other illegally confiscated hair appliances such as the Holy Curling Iron, the Blessed Hair Dryer, or the Really Cool Hair Braider. Claiming Palestine's actions amount to a crime against humanity, Israeli spokesman Caroline Sutton, fourteen, countered with a diplomatic, "Your hair is ugly and you're stupid and no boy would ever want to go out with you." Upon hearing that, twelve-year-old Palestinian leader Katie Sutton retaliated with a torrent attack on Israel, bitch slapping its door, stealing its hairbrush, and vowing never to return Israel's hair bands. Israel threatened to detain Palestine's new bra and the dress for the dance that somehow happened to end up in its room—honest, Israel doesn't know how that happened—to which Palestine countered with the threat of withholding the detained purse, scarf, and twenty-two dollars Israel inadvertently left on the couch the night before when it fell asleep watching an episode of CSI. These events came as long-suffering UN delegates Ellen and Kevin tried in vain to stem the tide of petty violence that has ravaged this area for as long as anyone can remember, and longer than anyone should have to endure, if you really must know. Israel, however, says a blockade will be a necessary security measure to stem the salvos of insults and really hurtful name-calling that have been fired by the Palestinian rebels into its area, which includes the bedroom, the occupied territories of the computer room, the Holy Land (otherwise known as the bathroom), and Israel's side of the family room couch, adding, "I wish Palestine would quit looking at me" and the all-too-familiar, "Hey, Palestine's foot touched my leg, tell it to stop." More as this story unfolds. We now return to our regularly scheduled letter already in progress.* —which is how a bill becomes a law. And

2008 was also a historic year for women born from white mothers, as for the first time ever a Sutton girl left home and went out on her own. Beth, at twenty-two, got out of college, out of the house, and moved out to Columbus, Georgia, working for Aflac. Yes, the company with the stupidly annoying spokesduck. One day it occurred to Kevin and Ellen why she took a job there. You know the Stockholm syndrome, where a hostage begins identifying with its captors? Same principle. After growing up in the Sutton household, she just got used to being surrounded by a whole lot of annoying. If she gets really homesick, she can simply add to the Aflac duck an eardrum-piercing siren, a twenty-four-hour Kanye West/Akon marathon, any movie by Hannah Montana, the soundtrack to MTV's *My Super Sweet 16*, a toenail (unclipped) scratching across a chalkboard, and the sound of Katie in the morning when she cannot find her school ID. Just tap your heels together twice and say, "There's no place like seven-hundred-thirty-nine-point-ninety-three miles from home." Also, 2008 was the year Kevin stupidly bought Julie a Vespa. It's like a motorcycle, but less safe. Julie, nineteen, a sophomore and Kappa Alpha Theta at Indiana University, called her dad every day from January 1 to June 29 on the phone. Every day she asked how he was doing. Every day she laughed at his jokes— even the one that was funny. Every day she told him he was witty and handsome and, oh, she really, really, really wanted a Vespa. So finally, on June 29, Kevin caved in and got her one. June 29 was the last time Julie has spoken to him. "Frankly, after he bought me that Vespa, and if the tuition is paid, I try to have as little contact with those people as possible," Julie probably recently said. "I mean, why do you think I went out of state? I had to get as far away as I could, plus that out-of-state tuition really sticks it to my dad. I remember that time I was six years old and I wanted this doll at Toys"R"Us and he didn't let me get it, and I remember how much I cried in the back seat all the way home. Well, who's crying in the back seat now, Dad?" Kevin knows who's cry— *And now this special news break from the Middle East. Early morning conflicts escalated when it was learned that other adversaries of Israel have now joined the heated clash. Julie Sutton, a nineteen-year-old twin currently away at college, has also claimed Israel has raided her closet and worn an unauthorized dress. Israeli officials described Julie as "a hotbed for terrorist preparations" and claim that more than two hundred harsh words had been fired from there in the past four weeks. Julie countered with a barrage of strategically placed I-Did-Not-Say-You-Could-Wear-My-Dress bombs, after which a series of Yes-You-Did and No-I-Didn't surface-to-ear missiles were volleyed. Julie has currently retreated to her sorority house where she can, from 883 miles away, somehow remain keenly aware of exactly what has been touched, and by whom, in her bedroom. Late last week, Israel's ambassador Caroline said it was committed to building on successes in human rights and dealing with any shortcomings, and welcomed a "positive and productive" dialogue with the Palestinian people. Then she kicked Palestine in the back seat of the Suburban, saying, "The mighty rains of Allah are upon you." Or maybe it was, "You are a lying liar, and give me back my hairbrush." The start of December saw the official launch of a peace proposal that Israeli and Palestinian officials have been working on for the past two and a half years. The hope is for a lasting peace. Time will tell if that comes to fruition. And now, back to our regularly scheduled Christmas letter, in progress.* —and that is the infield fly rule. And 2008 was also the year Kelly got a tattoo. Yes, like wiping a booger on the *Mona Lisa*, Kelly, nineteen, a sophomore at Texas State, got a tattoo. Yes, the girl with the 3.91 GPA got herself a permanent Chinese symbol that translates into English as, "Me poke sharp stick into father's heart long time." Yes, the president of her dorm just became eligible to be a regular on *Cops*. Yes, the vice president of the university French Club and member of the Sigma Alpha Lambda honors fraternity got herself a Britney Spears starter kit. Kelly was recently selected to study abroad next semester in France, land of hairy armpits, nose rings, poodles and, worst of all, French people. What wonders lie in store for Kevin when she returns? He can only— *Once again we interrupt this letter to bring you an update on the Middle East peace accord. After just four minutes, the much-anticipated peace proposal that Israeli and Palestinian officials had brokered the past two and a half years is officially over. The latest breakout in hostilities occurred when it was discovered that Israel had been on the computer for twenty-two minutes playing SIMS while Palestine was allowed to be on for only twenty-one minutes and twenty-nine seconds. Oh, the inequities of life. The war rages on.*

Officials do not know what the future holds for peace in this region, but one thing is for sure. They sure are loud. They sure are annoying. They sure are stupid. And this sure gets old. And now, back to our regularly scheduled letter already in progress. — and then Kevin said, "And that wasn't my finger." So as 2008 comes to an end, Kevin and Ellen ask: was this our stupidest year ever? Considering the depression, the war, the mortgage crisis, the stock market meltdown, bailouts, American auto executives, global warming, the Vespa, the tattoo, the angry chorus line, the duck, Caroline slamming the dog's tail in the car door, and the tragedy of having one straightening iron for two girls, considering all that, maybe Caroline was right. But, as Barack Obama said, it's time for change. Until that happens, Ellen is stuck with Kevin. So, as we wrap up this 2008 let— *This just in. It is 1:30 a.m. local time. Peace has fallen on this war-torn region in the early hours when both Israel and Palestine finally, finally, finally went to bed. Who knows what the morning will bring, especially with the news that Palestine has "recovered" the Sacred Straightening Iron and hidden it under her pillow.*

Merry Christmas and a much less stupid 2009 from the Suttons: Ellen, Kevin, Beth, Julie, Kelly, Caroline, and Katie.

Intelligence is what separates us from the apes.
—Charles Darwin

Learning is stupid.
—Caroline Sutton

2009

Sorry, there will be no letter this year.

Due to the economy and the resulting severe budget cuts, and a bad case of prickly heat, the annual year-end Sutton Family Christmas Letter® that you have become so accustomed to throwing away the very moment it arrives will not be coming this year. We would like to apologize to any landfill owners who were looking forward to reaching their yearly quota, but severe economic conditions will force you to look elsewhere for other sources of trash. (Hey, how about TMZ's nonstop Tiger Woods coverage?) This year's letter was going to be entitled "OUR KEVINLY FATHER." You would have chuckled at its cleverness and yet been slightly put off by its hint of sacrilege. Oh, the humor that would have ensued. The title, "OUR KEVINLY FATHER," would have been blared out in the same comfortably familiar big letters (Arial Regular font, forty-two point) across the top of the page as in years past. But, due to cutbacks at headquarters, that will not happen this year. As part of a last-ditch effort to save this year's letter, the boys in corporate got together and proposed a money-saving idea to increase the point size of this year's letter, which would allow the letter's writer to give you fewer words in the same amount of space. Sort of the publishing industry's equivalent to when you open a huge bag of potato chips and there are only, like, two measly chips in the bag and you realize you just paid a dollar ninety-nine for mostly air. But, when you think about it, you pay a dollar for water in a bottle when that exact same water comes out of a tap pretty much free, so maybe you enjoy being ripped off. If that is the case, a deposed Nigerian prince needs you to deposit a thousand dollars into a special account for only a few hours so he can transfer forty million dollars out of his country, and for your efforts you will be rewarded handsomely. Oh, and that prince's name is Kevin Sutton. Diversions out of left field such as the previous story will also not happen this year, also victim of the recession. Plus, because of major cutbacks in every department, there will be zero chance this year of a tpyo—welcome as a mime—sneaking into the letter. And, since there won't be a letter, there won't be the chance of you reading along when suddenly and for no apparent reason the sentence you are reading somehow just abruptlyThat will not happen this year, yet another victim of these economic times. There will be none of Kevin's Nobel Prize-considered observations about living with a wife and five daughters, even though it's down to four because Beth smartly moved out and lives on her own in Columbus, Georgia, and mostly down to two daughters because Julie is a junior and away at Indiana University and Kelly is a junior and away at Texas State, but still the wife and the two daughters Kevin currently retains are equal to three wives and twelve daughters at any exchange rate in any economy. Due to budget cuts, you will not hear the story of what recently happened when Ellen and Caroline were screaming at each other at the tops of their lungs about something only a human without testicles would scream about, or even waste non-baseball-watching time caring about, when Caroline (fifteen and in tenth grade) came to Kevin looking for a sympathetic ally and asked him, "What is wrong with Mom? Why is she being like that?" Due to the recession, you will not discover that Kevin responded with, "Because she's a woman, Caroline, and you are still a girl. You'll be maddeningly unreasonable soon enough yourself. It just takes time. You see, the lion eats the zebra, Caroline. It's nature. The lion does not pass value judgments on the zebra or stop and consider the zebra's lot in life. The lion sees the zebra, the lion eats the zebra. Pure and simple." Downsizing at corporate will prevent you from reading Caroline's subsequent one-word response, the simple but timeless, "Whatever," which was coupled with the perfectly choreographed eye roll that Kevin has deciphered over the years to be teenage-girl shorthand code for, "Whatever...you say is obviously a brilliant observation of humankind, Dad, and I am sure you would one day be recognized for the genius you are if you didn't live among savages." That story, alas, will not be told. Blame the economy. Nor will you discover the classic

Carolineism she hatched when asked why her grades in English were slipping, and she responded with, "I know the answers to everything I'm not asked, I just don't know the answers to the questions I am asked." Also, you will not hear about the time Katie (thirteen and in eighth grade) came storming down the stairs on a school day at 8:05, still in her pajamas, screaming at 100 percent FEMALE (Full Estrogen Mode and Loudly Ear-bursting), "I AM LATE FOR SCHOOL AND IT'S ALL YOUR FAULT, DAD. NOBODY WOKE ME UP FOR SCHOOL." Kevin ever so gently reminded her, "What do you mean? Your mom woke you up a half hour ago when you got a phone call." To which Katie responded, "SHE WOKE ME UP FOR A PHONE CALL, BUT NOBODY WOKE ME UP FOR SCHOOL." That story will not be told this year. Nor will the story about Julie and Kelly and the bitterly cold day in January when they were running late for a nail appointment. (One can only guess that their nailologist has a packed schedule and being late would throw the entire nail-grooming industry off-kilter.) That particular day just happened to be the coldest morning in Dallas in about fifteen years, a morning where the outside temperature was twelve degrees. But, they were in a hurry. Oftentimes people in a hurry absent-mindedly leave the front door unlocked. But Kevin and Ellen's overachieving twins cannot do things like normal human XX-chromosome life forms. No, they didn't leave the house in a hurry and leave the door unlocked on this, the coldest day in Dallas. They left the house in a hurry and left the front door open. Open. Yes, open. As in the same position Kevin's mouth fell into and remained in for a good ten minutes after he heard what they had done. They left the front door wide open. On the coldest day of the year. Were the pets gone? Yes, but they came back (even the cats, dammit). Was anything stolen? Not a single computer or TV or strand of jewelry (the Sacred Straightening Iron hasn't been spotted in a while, though, and Caroline swears she doesn't know where it is). But something did come up missing. A huge chunk of money from Kevin's bank account because he had to buy a new furnace. Due to the budget cuts, you will not be privy to this invaluable tip Kevin was going to pass along as a public service: If you or someone you love (or are legally compelled to love) is planning on leaving the front door completely wide open on the coldest day of the year, be advised that the average high-efficiency furnace is not rated to heat a city of 2.4 million people. Perhaps if the economy rebounds next year, Kevin can pass on that tidbit to you. After all, it is just a bit of tid. How much could that cost? Since there will be no letter this year, you also will not enjoy one of Kevin's classic lists, like the year he listed the disgusting things he found on Caroline's floor, many of which, by the way, are still there or have mutated into new life forms. This year's list would have been about one of the all-time classic parent pet peeves: The late-night, last-minute, are-you-kidding-me, eleven-o'clock reminder of things the kids need for school in the morning but don't have and really, really need: 1) Tennis balls. 2) A bag of feathers—who knew feathers were (a) sold in bags, and (b) sold at all? 3) A yellow calculator. 4) A pony. 5) A ten-pound bag of sand; must be at least 75 percent silica based. 6) A math book left at school (but if it's already at school, then why are you telling us, at 11:47 at night, that you need to bring it to school?). 7) A cake. 8) Frosting. 9) Those little things, not sure what they are called, that you put on the cake, oh yeah, sprinkles, but they need to be gold and purple or I will flunk. 10) Poster board. 11) It has to be twenty-four inches by thirty-six inches. 12) It has to be gold. 13) With graph lines. Sadly, you will now be deprived of things such as that. Cutbacks are tough on everyone. (Note to anyone willing to open a twenty-four-hour Bag of Feathers store: Kevin would have gladly given you one hundred thousand dollars that night, no questions asked.) Any and all efforts were made to continue the tradition of a year-end letter, but in the end, it just was not economically feasible. What, in this economy? Maybe next year. If the stimulus package goes through. Or the prickly heat disappears. (It's really not the rash that is so bothersome; it's the swelling and itching.) All efforts will be made to make it worth the wait.

To everyone who was a victim of the recession and lost a job, lost considerable amounts of savings, or lost sixteen hundred dollars on the coldest day of the year in Dallas in 2009, we would like to wish you a Merry Christmas and a Happy New Year (because the new one cannot possibly be worse than the old one). From Kevin, Ellen, Beth, Julie, Kelly, Caroline, and Katie Sutton.

And thanks to Jay the dog for coming back home that cold, cold day in January. You thought it was going to be warmer back at the house, but you were wrong. Stupid dog.

2010

Ellen and Kevin are splitting up.

The year 2010 was a landmark year in the Sutton household, with plenty of surprising ups and downs and twists and turns. The most significant happening, however, comes totally out of left field to everyone who has known Ellen and Kevin throughout their twenty-seven years of marriage. In a staggering development nobody would have ever foreseen, it is with great shock and surprise that we make this major announcement to all our friends and loved ones: Julie and Kelly are graduating from college. That's right, the biggest news in 2010 from Ellen and Kevin (aside from the fact that Kevin's vasectomy is still holding strong after fourteen years, although that surgery's success doesn't get tested as often as statistically necessary for accurate scientific validation, which means the term *holding strong* takes on a whole different context) are the upcoming graduations of Julie and Kelly from college. Kelly from Texas State on December 17, Julie from Indiana University on December 18. Yes, Kelly on Friday evening, Julie on Saturday morning. Born fifteen minutes apart, graduating fifteen hours apart. Making it physically impossible for Kevin and Ellen to attend both. Kevin's suggestion? Pick the favorite one and go to hers. Ellen, as always, had a different suggestion. "Why don't we split up?" Upon hearing that, Kevin immediately pulled out all the elementary school directories and started circling the hot moms in the neighborhood, until he realized that by "split up" Ellen simply meant just for the weekend's graduation festivities.

So as mid-December ambles along, and as the directories are stored away once again, Kevin and Ellen are headed to two different graduations in two different parts of the country. Kevin to San Marcos, Texas; Ellen to Bloomington, Indiana. It's been a long, strange trip for Julie and Kelly to get to this point. Kevin and Ellen still remember the time when Julie and Kelly were four years old and in preschool and a girl in their class was a big bully to them. Every day they would come home crying. Ellen would always try to pass along gentle wisdom like, "You know, girls, a bully is just a person who really hates herself inside." Kevin's wisdom at times like these didn't apply at a time like this: "Punch them in the testicles." So one day the twins came up with a plan. A brilliantly vengeful, XX-chromosomian plan. And they were only four. Julie bit Kelly's arm—hard. Kelly cried. Kelly bit Julie's arm— hard. Julie cried. They both cried and cried and cried. Their preschool teacher asked them what was wrong. They showed their bite marks to the teacher, deep bite marks. Then they said that the bully girl had done this to them. The bully girl was kicked out of preschool. Moral of the story: When life bites you, bite back. Hard. And leave marks. There was also that one time Kelly and Kevin were at the kitchen table playing cards when the twins were younger. They were about seven, eight, nine, somewhere in that range. It was in the summer, or maybe the fall, though it might have been spring. It might have been late at night, might have been just after dinner. Mind you, this was more than a decade ago, so details are sketchy. Kevin was beating Kelly 485 to 260 in Rummy 500. Julie came downstairs in her nightgown, which was no big deal. She said hello to Kevin in a sweet, almost loving tone of voice. Hmmm, something was up. She walked past Kelly without so much as a half bitch slap. Hmmm, something was very, very up. Then she walked out toward the garage. Very, very, very odd. "Hey, Julie," Kevin asked, "where are you going?" *"To the bathroom,"* she replied. Oh, OK. Wait, did we just hear what we thought we heard? To the bathroom? Kevin dropped his cards and ran into the garage after her. Kelly sneaked a peek at Kevin's hand, then followed suit by following him out. They threw open the door leading into the garage. Julie was peeing. In the freezer. And it was at that precise moment that Kevin and Ellen discovered Julie sleepwalked. It was also the moment that the lemonade ice cubes suddenly became less of a special treat. Not only did Julie sleepwalk, she also awakewalked. Perhaps you recall the story of when Julie was six and drew a picture for Ellen and Kevin. A picture of a horse. To be more precise, and to be fair to horses, it looked more like a raccoon that had been flattened by a rolling pin and then was subsequently flattened by a steamroller, and then had a fluffy tail stuck willy-nilly onto its lower back, and legs that totally violated the ball-and-socket principle. Julie was proud of it. Kevin felt sorry for her. He gave her a quarter for the drawing, and Julie ran up to her room, clutching her quarter, out of sight for the afternoon. Ellen and Kevin duly thanked God for that. A few hours later, a call came in from a neighbor down the street. It seemed Julie was going door-to-door selling drawings of semiflattened quadruped-challenged raccoon-horses for a quarter apiece. She had already earned four dollars and seventy-five cents. It's amazing how much people will pay for crap. A fact that has kept Kevin gainfully employed for twenty-nine years. Yet those same two girls, Julie and Kelly, somehow found a way to graduate from college. In three and a half years. Kelly will graduate summa cum laude, which is Latin for, "Surprise, you are now officially off the company dole, when can you start making that car payment?" And 2010 was also the year Caroline turned sixteen and became a junior in high school. She got a car. She named it Charlie. She drives around with a miniature pumpkin on the dashboard. She named the pumpkin Stuart. Why? Because she is sixteen and a junior in high school. One day, after pitching lessons, she was driving back with Kevin in her car. Her radio was playing. Kevin, ever possessing the golden voice of a Greek god (scratch that, Greek dog), started singing. Caroline flashed her "Ellen Look" at him. You know the look. Just be married to Ellen for twenty-seven years, say something wildly funny and witty and charming and always situationally appropriate, then immediately gaze at her. *That* look. Anyway, Kevin was singing in Caroline's car. What a festive mood he had set. Caroline remained silent for a minute or two, then she calmly asked, "Hey, Dad, who sings this song?" Kevin, feeling good that he could impress his daughter with his in-depth knowledge of mid-2000s pop music, replied, *"It's Coldplay."* "Why don't we just leave it that way then, OK?" And, in one chilling moment, so chilling Julie could pee on it, Caroline showed that Julie and Kelly weren't the only ones who were masters of biting.

But sarcasm isn't Caroline's strongest skill. That would be sleeping. No man, woman, or child alive can sleep with the intensity, determination, joy, and sheer volume of hours as Rip Van Caroline. She slept her whole freshman year of high school, half her sophomore year, and the entire months of June and July this summer. The same week Caroline took a vicious line drive to her forehead in a softball game and went to the hospital with a concussion, Katie also had to go to the hospital. Katie is a freshman in high school, a volleyball player, a guitar player, a horseback rider, a baby-sitter, a choir singer, and a cheerleader. Turns out there is one thing she is not, though. Made of rubber. During cheerleading practice, they tossed Katie in the air in a brilliantly executed fly move. The catch move was, however, not so brilliantly executed. Katie landed on her elbow. On the hard gym floor. It has been proven throughout history that the gym floor mostly wins in that contest. Katie broke her elbow. The time off from volleyball gave her ample time to think of new ways to annoy Caroline. The two got into this fight, almost verbatim: "We don't fight as much as we used to." *"Yes, we do, we fight more."* "No, we don't, we fight a lot less, and you're an idiot if you don't agree." *"We fight a lot more, but you're too stupid to see that."* "You're the stupid one, we don't fight nearly as much as we used to. And that's only because you're not as annoying as you used to be." Honest to God, they actually got into a fight about not fighting. We are not sure who won, but are 100 percent certain who lost: humanity, reason, common sense, and Kevin and Ellen. Beth is still living in Columbus, Georgia, and still working for Aflac. She is an operations analyst. That is just fancy corporate-speak for analyzing operations. Recently Beth got a new cat, which means, of course, soon Kevin and Ellen will be getting a new cat. To go with the other cat Beth used to have. Here's one thing Kevin doesn't get about cats. Or about women. Women get all— perhaps the most appropriate word to use here would be pissy— with guys about the whole bathroom, toilet seat, missing the target, maybe forgetting occasionally to flush business. For that, men are mocked and scorned and told they are animals and exiled to the far reaches of the bed. Yet, these same women take absolute and utter delight in a pet whose only discernible reason for existence is to crap in a sandbox in the open in the house. And for that, they are petted and loved and told they are little darlings and allowed to snuggle with them at night. So Kevin is trying an experiment. While Ellen is currently away on the other side of the country at Julie's graduation, Kevin has decided to leave a surprise in the little sandbox thingy for her when she gets back home. Oh, the anticipation of the petting, the loving, and the unbridled admiration he will receive upon her return! Well, that was 2011 in the Sutton house, where right this very minute Kevin is apologizing to Ellen, seeing as how this is the first time she had not been around to authorize and approve the contents of the annual Sutton Family Christmas Letter, and he is very, very sorry for that "following suit" pun in the card game story. Such a cheap, easy pun is in no way appropriate for a Christmas letter. (Oh, there it is. The Ellen Look.)

Merry Christmas and Happy New Year from Kevin, Ellen, Beth, Julie, Kelly, Caroline, and Katie Sutton. Oh, and enjoy the lemon ICEEs.

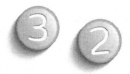

THE STUFF OF LEGEND

After a while, you just stop getting on girls for living like pigs. Life is too short to worry about things like that.

On my deathbed, I don't think I will really give a damn whether my daughters didn't make their beds for twelve years straight.

But I drew the line at leaving their crap around the house. They can live in Boone County, West Virginia, if they want, but I am not going to.

Whatever they left lying around outside their sties, I would toss into the garage. They would get so angry with me: "Dad, that blouse cost two hundred dollars. How can you just throw it in the garage? There are cockroaches and oil stains out there."

I would pick up their hundred-dollar boots and show them just how easy it is to throw something in the garage.

It's really very easy. Try it.

I would be willing to bet they'd find cockroaches and oil stains on their own bedroom floors if they had any way of finding their floors.

Caroline was the worst. We had hoped common decency would eventually force her to clean her room, that when she had friends come over, she would clean it for them out of embarrassment, but that didn't happen.

Her friends who would sleep over would just sleep on a couch. I bet most of them had no idea Caroline even had a bed in her room anyway.

Caroline's room was so monumentally messy, it was finally immortalized in an ad.

A photographer friend of mine was looking for a location to shoot an image for an ad on teenage scoliosis. The headline of the ad read: "We can straighten her spine, which is more than we can promise about her room."

He told me he needed a messy room, and was probably going to have to fake one in a studio, but really didn't have money to pay for that.

I told him to come to my house and look at Caroline's room.

"No, this one has to be really messy."

I told him to come to my house and look at Caroline's room.

"No, almost comically messy. Like the kind of thing no human being would ever really live in."

I told him to come to my house and look at Caroline's room.

"No, I'm thinking trailer park pigsty meets garbage hoarder after Hurricane Katrina."

I told him to come to my house and look at Caroline's room.

The next morning, I met him at my house so he could scout her room.

"How long did it take you to do this?" he asked me, assuming I had faked it.

"Me? I didn't do this."

"There is no way any human being would ever live like that."

"Honest, I just opened the door. This is how it is."

He told me that if he tried to prop a messy room himself, he would have never come up with anything like it. "This is the mother lode of messy teenager rooms."

All we did was turn a few shoe boxes at an angle so you couldn't read their logos, we put Katie's guitar on the bed for a little more visual interest, and I moved a bulletin board from one wall where it wouldn't be seen to where it could be seen in the photo, since it had her name on it and I wanted Caroline's name in the ad for proof.

My photographer friend clicked and clicked and clicked to his heart's delight. He could not believe his luck.

Of course, when Caroline came home that night, she was furious that we ruined her room. I couldn't stop laughing. All we did was turn a few shoe boxes.

"But those were where they were supposed to be."

A few weeks later I showed her the ad. She was proud of it. Until word got around among her friends that it was her room in that ad.

A few days later, Caroline cleaned her room. It took nearly a week. Hazmat crews were called in. Soil experts showed up. NASA was there. Animal control stopped by.

The secret to raising girls? Forget it. Peer pressure is the answer to most things.

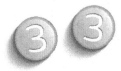

MILLION-DOLLAR IDEA

With five human leeches constantly sucking every last drop of financial blood out of me, I am constantly, desperately, thinking of million-dollar ideas to keep up with the staggering cost of these forced transfusions.

The prospects of paying for five college tuitions and five weddings will make a man's mind go to strange places. Here is one detour mine has taken recently. (I am looking for financial backers, by the way.)

I do a lot of business travel. Living in a household of women, it occurred to me one day that it's time for new thinking in shuttle services.

Women are a huge untapped market in business traveler passengers. But the fact is, most cabs and shuttle services are geared to men and haven't changed since the 1950s, when most businessmen were actually men.

The other fact is, most men really don't give a damn about things like cleanliness and hygiene and staphylococcus infections. They are guided by the misguided belief that the purpose of a cab ride is to merely get you from Point A to Point B.

A hairy driver picks you up in a dumpy, grimy cab and then talks your ear off nonstop about sports or politics or death to Christian infidels in the thickest of undetectable accents. Plus he smells like fermented falafel secretion.

Many businessmen today, however, are actually women who find such things distasteful.

So I had an idea.

What about a car service geared toward women where the drivers are all Chippendale dancers? Just like a standard car service, they drive her where she needs to go. And, just like standard cab drivers, they are shirtless.

But unlike a standard car service, instead of talking, the driver listens.

As the female passenger (and, I might add, paying customer) prattles on and on and on and on about the kinds of things women prattle on and on and on and on about—which, from my experience, are: 1) comparative butt sizes, 2) asshole guys, 3) hair and hair removal, 4) bitchy co-workers, 5) shoes, 6) jewelry, 7) vaginal discharges—the driver is instructed to act like he is listening intently to what she is saying.

Every ninety-two seconds he must respond with one of the preapproved FCIPs (Female Contentment-Inducing Phrases) of his choosing:

"I'm listening, please go on."

"You're kidding, she actually said that?"

"Yes, indeed, men are such jerks."

"Where did you get those shoes?"

"Did you do something with your hair?"

"She is such a bitch."

"I totally see your point."

"How was your day?" (Warning: only to be used on trips of seven hours or longer.)

"That sounds interesting, tell me more."

"You are good in math."

As I said, the cars will be driven by shirtless Chippendale dancers. The cars will be clean. The cars will smell like vanilla lavender.

Oh, and I'm going to call the company Shuttlecocks®.

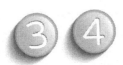

QUIT TELLING ME WHAT TO DO

This happened to me while trying to get a simple phone number from my iPhone.

ME: Siri, call the Angelika Theater.

SIRI: There are thirty-five movie theaters in your area, which would you like?

ME: Ahhhh, the ANGELIKA Theater, like I said.

SIRI: I am sorry, I cannot seem to find a listing for Angie's Cup Cakes.

ME: I said, "Angelika Theater."

SIRI: There are five Anglican churches in your area. Would you like me to show you the closest one?

ME: What I would like, Siri, is for you to GIVE ME THE PHONE NUMBER FOR THE ANGELIKA THEATER.

SIRI: There are no Argentinian barbers nearby. Would you like me to make an appointment for you?

ME: Wait a second. If there aren't any Argentinian barbers nearby, how can you make me an appointment? Look, what I'd really like you to do right now, Siri, is to go straight to Hell.

SIRI: Do you need travel times for Hell, Michigan?

ME: You suck, Siri.

SIRI: I have found one Angelika Theater near Yuma.

Steve Jobs created some of the most amazing technology of our lifetime.

Perhaps his most remarkable achievement is Siri, a machine that duplicates the logic of women with eerie precision.

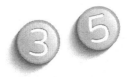

LETTING THEM GO

The most rewarding thing for a father is seeing your daughter walk out that door as a woman, recognizing you have done all you can to put your indelible stamp on her life and her personality, and realizing how lucky you are that she mostly takes after her mother.

One of my favorite phrases ever is something Caroline coined when describing our family: "Stupid stupidity." As a father, I simply tried to teach my girls to follow their own path and avoid stepping in the stupid stupidity.

Honestly, I just wanted them to be interesting.

In high school, out of the blue, Beth decided she wanted to take up diving, a sport that nobody even knew existed until then. She was quite good at it.

When she graduated, she earned a very substantial college scholarship not based on grades (although hers were good) but on her integrity. The pride I felt almost made me forget about her throwing up in my mouth.

She got a college degree in something that is very unusual for women—math. I am not saying women can't do math, I am saying women don't do math. Not too many women earn degrees in the field. If you think I'm being sexist, do the math. Or have a guy do the math for you. (OK, that might have been a tad sexist, but you forced me into it.)

Julie wanted to be a toilet for Halloween one year, so we took a trip to the Home Depot plumbing department and to the arts and crafts store, and she went as a toilet. She opened the lid and they tossed candy into the bowl. It's the most original Halloween costume I have ever seen. I'm proud that she didn't want to be just another ghost.

She also didn't want to go to the same junior high school as all her friends and her other sisters, and picked a small private school that was better suited for her. I'm proud of that. Proud and a lot broker.

If there was ever a kid with a true moral compass, it's Julie. She is a good person. She's devoted to helping children, and to me there is no greater cause in the world.

Kelly is an explorer. She's lived in France for a time, and likes to travel. In high school, she liked traveling out of the house at one in the morning through the back window.

She had a role in high school that was perfect for her outgoing personality: the team mascot. She patrolled the sidelines at high school football games in the big Wildcat costume and entertained the crowd as she pranked the players and coaches during games, doing things like getting on all fours right behind a player so when he took a step back he'd fall on his butt, tapping a player on the far shoulder pad and then acting like she didn't do it as he turned to see who tapped him, tickling the coach with the Wildcat tail and then ducking behind someone else when he tried to figure out what was going on. Mind you, this took guts. This is high school football in Texas. This is messing with religion.

I forgot how boring watching a football game is live. It's like going to the horse track. You place a bet, watch a few seconds of action, wait around doing nothing for half an hour, place a bet, watch a few seconds of action, wait around doing nothing for half an hour. Football is like fatherhood. A whole lot of standing around waiting for something to happen. Kelly did the impossible. She made football, and fatherhood, enjoyable.

On her own, Caroline applied and was accepted into a totally different high school than my other daughters, where she could dance. If ever anyone danced to the beat of a different drummer, it was Caroline.

Her dance teacher told her that if she was on the dance squad in high school, then that was the only extracurricular activity she could do.

So, using her best obeying skills, she also was the starting pitcher on the varsity softball team. Caroline and no are not acquainted.

Katie learned how to play guitar when she was in fourth grade and immediately wrote a song that made it to the finals of a statewide competition.

She would drive us nuts on long car trips with her ability to recall arcane details. We used to play what we called the alphabet game. One person would pick a random letter and say, "I'm thinking of an animal that starts with *S*." Then the others would shout out guesses. Whoever got it right first got to ask the next question. Before Katie got old enough to play, the rest of us suffering from stupid stupidity would pick animals like squirrel or skunk, or maybe something a bit more challenging like sloth. Katie's animals were always the most obscure names ever, like spectral bat or serval, which is an African wildcat that only African wildcat scholars and Katie had ever heard of.

Nobody makes me laugh more than Katie.

I don't write this as a way to brag on my kids, but to say that I am proud that they developed the ability to think on their own, to question things. Many times what they questioned were decisions Ellen or I made. That made for some challenging parenting, but nobody said it was supposed to be easy. I want them to have a point of view.

I want them to think on their own so they don't let stupid stupidity get in their way.

The world is filled with stupid stupidity.

Unfortunately, there comes a time when they have to leave home and go out into that stupid world, whether it's for college or for good. It's a sad day.

But if there is only one piece of advice you heed from me, make it this: get her a good set of luggage as a going-away gift.

In time, you will realize how practical this advice really will become.

Truth is, that suitcase is going to be all you will see of her from here on out. When she comes back for weekends or holidays, it's really her luggage that comes home to spend time with you. She ends up spending every hour going to see her friends.

That suitcase is her stand-in for any and all family functions from now on. Get good luggage.

Of course, you can still have those family dinners you have been pining to have, like when she was younger. It will be with her suitcase, however, and not with her. It will probably be much like the family dinners you remember, but with slightly less grunting.

Family dinner conversation before:

You: "So, how was school today?"

Her: "(Unintelligibly aloof mumble.)"

Family dinner conversation now:

You: "So, how are things going?"

Her luggage: "   ."

I have found that, chances are, her luggage doesn't ask to borrow your car to go see her friends, or for money to go out with them.

Good luggage.

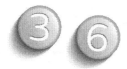

GROWING GIRLS

What do I know about women? As far as I can tell, about as much as the Lifetime Network or *Cosmopolitan*. Seriously, how many secrets to a flat tummy can they really know?

I have a mom and three sisters and a wife and five daughters. That makes me as much of an expert as the experts.

I remember one particular time when a woman running an advertising account told me I couldn't work on the assignment because, as a guy, I didn't know the "female point of view."

That made me laugh.

Hey, I was the guy who came up with the genius idea for a feminine hygiene client to increase sales and brand loyalty with an instant-win game, where women could win up to a million dollars instantly every time they bought a box of Kotex. It was called "The Rags to Riches Game."

And I don't know women?

I said to her, "Look, I grew up with four of you. I came out of one of you. I married one of you. I made five of you. I'm like the female factory. You are getting this insight factory-direct."

She dismissed me as if I were a heterosexual interior designer. "You don't know the female point of view."

"Oh, so you're saying all women think alike? This should be easy, then," I reasoned. It was a darn solid reasoning, too.

"No, I'm *not* saying all women think alike at all."

"But you just said there's a female point of view. That implies there is just one, which implies all women think the same, doesn't it?"

"No."

"So, then, there *isn't* a female point of view?"

"Well, yes and no."

"What is it? Yes, all women think alike so there's a female point of view? Or no, all women don't think alike so there's not a female point of view?"

She angrily shot back, "You're twisting my words all out of context."

"I *knew* you were going to say that," I replied. "Hey, maybe I *do* get the female point of view. It's to get angry when you're wrong and you don't get your way."

She walked away mad. Just like I knew she would.

My duty as a father was to ensure that at least five of their species possessed some semblance of common sense and reason and logic.

The one thing I know is, raising girls is tough. It's even tougher today when crap like Lady Gaga gets passed off as something young girls should aspire to. Or when something like Facebook allows their reputations to be ruined forever, instantly, and more widespread than the old way—by the mean girls in high school.

Help them discover a moral compass and make yourself their role model instead of Lindsay Lohan and this will be a much better world for all of us.

The hardest thing for any parent—and many female advertising executives—to understand is that each girl is totally different.

It is truly baffling. *This* one came from me and my wife, and *that* one came from me and that same wife, yet *this* one is sneaking out the back window to meet friends at one in the morning, and *that* one could be a nun the minute she masters the intricacies of smacking a kid on the wrist with a yardstick.

Don't be alarmed when you think you've done everything right, then on the day she turns thirteen aliens snatch her away and replace her with a functionally insane exact lookalike of your daughter. The aliens bring her back on her nineteenth birthday.

I started thinking about writing this book the day I dropped off Caroline at college. The long nine-hour ride back home got me thinking about what a long road it was getting her there.

My first three daughters all excelled in school. They graduated from college, in fact, in three and a half years. Academically, my youngest daughter excels as well.

So naturally, as parents, you cannot figure out why all your daughters aren't like that. It's the wrong way to think.

Caroline isn't like her sisters. She took to high school as Sarah Palin took to word readin'. It wasn't her thing. She was never motivated to do homework or study. She never seemed that interested.

What was especially frustrating was that she was the brightest of our kids. She spoke complete sentences right away, and had an uncanny memory. When she was five she told us she could recall what it was like being in her mother's belly. "Throw up would rain down on me like rocks."

While her indifference drove us nuts—especially since we didn't discover she had made the grades to graduate high school until the very last test of the very last day—on that drive home it occurred to me, that's OK.

Fatherhood comes with plenty of mistakes and lessons learned. That was one of them.

Even though high school didn't seem to motivate her, I could sense something different in her the moment she set foot on that college campus. For the first time in a long time, she seemed genuinely happy. I sensed an exhale. The pressure of high school and graduation were lifted. I was taken by a calming feeling that she is going to be fine. All that crap we agonized over didn't matter. Maybe it just took her a bit longer. She will do well in college.

It could very well be that being out of her house and sending her parents to the poorhouse was the root of her newfound happiness.

Shortly after, I saw a picture of her doing something I had never seen before. Studying at her desk.

But there was no denying she is totally different from her four sisters. Often, I was sure she was adopted. But you learn that they each develop at different paces, and that's OK.

Just four months earlier, I had the privilege of marrying off my first daughter.

As a father, what made me happiest about that entire ordeal wasn't the flowers or the dress or the menu at the reception or the heaping servings of Gentleman Jack on ice from the bar, or even the look of happiness on Beth's face that day.

It was the guy she was marrying. He is a great guy.

In spite of every mistake I'd made, every ball I'd dropped as a dad, every school play I'd missed, every deaf hot dog vendor I'd offended, somehow it all seemed to work. (Of course, a little of that could have been her mother's doing.)

It was my proudest day. So far.

As part of the task of being the father of the bride—once the wedding place confirms the check hasn't bounced—they let you give a toast to the new bride and groom.

What has always bugged me about weddings is this feeling of giddiness that comes over women, this foolish belief that it is "the happiest day of a woman's life."

Bullshit.

I started out by saying, "This is not the happiest day of your life. Why do people say that? How sad. If this is the happiest day of your life, then what do you have to look forward to? Is it all downhill from here?

"This should not be the happiest day of your life. This should just be the start of a lot of really good days *after* this. If you're lucky, this is a day you soon forget because all the rest of the days from here on out you are actually doing something with more meaning."

Then it was my time to make a toast. What I learned from being married to one of the truly great ones is that the secret to a marriage that lasts longer than the wedding cake is understanding that the person you are married to today isn't the person you will be married to tomorrow. People ebb and flow. Sometimes that person is a much better person tomorrow. Sometimes that person is a total pain in the ass tomorrow. But if you can adjust and not be selfish and not let the petty crap get to you and not worry about winning or losing and keeping score, things will work out and you will not have to give away half your assets.

So this was my toast:

> When you are an island
> I'll be the deep blue sea
> With love that is endless
> Wash over you and me
> When you are a pilot
> I'll be the open sky
> With love that's uplifting
> How high do you want to fly?
> When you are a desert
> I'll be a cool clear lake
> With love that is quenching
> Like rain on an early spring day
> When you're a tornado
> I'll be your four strong walls
> With love that's an oak tree
> Too strong to let you fall
> And when you are a candle

I'll be a gentle wind
That keeps the flame burning
With love that will never end
No matter who you are today
I'll be there for you anyway

I reprinted it here because my daughter wanted a copy of it. So now, Beth, when you buy this book, you will have it. Granted, it's not Shakespeare. But then again, he had only two daughters. Three more and the guy would have figured out that writing thing.

So here I am today. In the span of four months, I went from the financially crippling act of paying for a wedding to the financially crippling act of paying college tuition. With four more weddings and one more college tuition on the way.

We rejoin this bloodletting already in progress.

Driving through the empty prairies of the Midwest back home to Dallas, I had a lot of time to think. And it occurred to me, finally, after all these years, what the true secret to raising daughters is:

Abstinence. It makes the funds grow stronger.

And if you screw up that one, there's always Plan B:

Midol.

Stock up, buddy. It might just be the best pill ever invented for men. Even if it covers only one week a month.

2011

The night Caroline and Katie walked in on an intruder.

As another year's end comes chugging up on us (and if Ellen's surprise fiftieth birthday-party-slash-girls-weekend at the beach resort Isle of Palms was any indication, chugging is the appropriate word here), it's time for Kevin and Ellen to reflect on yet another twelve months of what they call "growing girls." Or, in the vernacular of the people, "hell." As always, it's not right to judge the entire 365 days of the year simply based on 364 of them. Because some days were worse than others. Far worse. Kevin, for instance, will never forget those screams of terror that winter night of July 11, 2011. "AHHHHHHHHHHHHHHHHHHHH! AHHHHHHHHHHHHHHHHHHHHHHHHHHHHHHHHHHHHHHHHHHH!" It was almost midnight, Dallas time. Caroline and Katie were downstairs watching television. Not PBS. They decided to go into the kitchen to get something to eat, because at that time there weren't enough dirty dishes strewn about the TV room to complete the Southwestern White Trash motif they were striving for. It suddenly turned very frightening. Because at that very moment, Caroline and Katie realized they were not alone downstairs. Their hearts stopped as they saw a shadowy figure dart through the living room and into the hallway. They froze. Utter, absolute panic took over. Not only were they unable to move, they were unable to form even the simplest of words. (Dear God, can you make that permanent?) It's well documented that deep fear can cause traumatic loss of motor skills. And, oddly, in some cases, motor homes. The best these poor defenseless girls could do at that moment was to scream out in absolute, unintelligible hysteria: "AHHHHHHHHHHHHHHHHHHHHHHHHH!" Kevin bolted up in bed. Problem was, the bed was some 5,200 miles away in Buenos Aires, Argentina. Kevin will never forget the feeling of helplessness that came over him that night in July, hearing his vulnerable daughters scream for their lives over the phone, with him so far away it was winter. As any father's would be in this situation, his first thought was, *How much is this call costing me?* But then he brushed away the cobwebs of international time zone changes and calling card rates, and set about trying to calm them down and figure out the best course of action, long-distance. Trouble was, their screaming was so hysterical, the best he could make out was a "HELLLP!" then a "HE'S...IN...THE...HALLWAY!" then another "HELLLP!" then a "MOM! UPSTAIRS! SLEEPING!" Piecing it together, Kevin asked, "OK, have you called nine-one-one?" Caroline replied, teary and trembling, "WILL THEY KILL HIM?" Kill him? *Kill* him? Kevin started to get really worried when suddenly, like spotting a man in a turban in midflight, the terror level spiked higher. "AHHHHHHHHHHHHHHHHHHHHHHHHH! HE'S BACK, DAD! HE'S BACK! AND HE JUST CRAWLED INTO THE LIVING ROOM!" Crawled? Did they say, crawled? "Wait a minute, girls, there's a burglar *crawling* through the house?" "NOOOOO, IT'S A BUG! KILL IT, DAD! IT'S HUGE AND IT'S GROSS AND IT'S ICKY!!!!!!" While there is no denying it must have been icky, seeing as how they used six exclamation points to describe its ickiness, and the internationally recognized standard in that usage is four, Kevin will never forget what happened next. He hung up the phone on them. Then he sat back in his bed, took a deep breath, and he prayed, "Dear God, please rescind Bernoulli's principle of air flow pressure differential so that the concept of air travel is no longer possible and I will be forced to live the rest of my life five thousand two hundred miles away in Argentina." When he woke up the next morning, he was thrilled to discover his prayers had been answered. For six more days. Kevin enjoyed his time spent in Argentina and learned many fascinating things about its people and their culture. For instance, unlike most people in the United States, Argentinian homeless can speak English. He discovered that as he was walking to a restaurant with a few colleagues. As they passed an Argentinian homeless man who was standing in front of one of the many Buenos Aires brothels, the homeless Argentine reached out a hand and asked Kevin, *"Excuse me, Americano, but can you lend me a couple of dollars so I can eat?"* Kevin sized up the situation, and asked, "How do I know you aren't going to just take that money and spend it inside there?" *"Oh, I have hooker money. I need food money."* One has to admire the Argentinian priority system. Evita would have been so proud. Kevin was also happy to have found the only bar in Buenos Aires that aired the Major League Baseball All-Star Game. A place called Remember El Alamo. It was a jam-packed, three-story sports bar that had fifty-five TVs showing South American Cup soccer and one TV showing American baseball. He sat near that TV. Right next to a British man with the thickest of Cockney accents. Just Kevin's luck that in a bar filled with a thousand Spanish-speaking people, he happened to sit next to the one person who spoke English and yet he could not understand a single word the man was saying. Later in the evening, a group of young Argentinians mistook Kevin for Ed O'Neill from *Modern Family* and insisted on buying him pitchers of beer, shouting, *"Mas cervesa* for *Modern Family. Mas cervesa* for *Modern Family."* After three pitchers, Kevin felt the honorable thing to do was to try to convince them he was not, in fact, Ed O'Neill. That was a four-pitcher-long conversation. Kevin's Spanish is rusty. His liver, however, is not. Unfortunately for Kevin, and for Ellen, Kevin eventually had to return home. When he walked into the house, he discovered one of Katie's unique new talents. Pest control. Kevin spotted a yellow Styrofoam bowl turned upside down and taped to the living room floor. "What the heck is that?" he asked Katie. *"That bug you wouldn't kill,"* she said coldly as she turned away, still angry six days later that Kevin refused to board the first flight out of Buenos Aires to perform his dadly duties. It seems Katie's revolutionary new system for killing bugs is the Suffocate Them Under a Styrofoam Bowl Method. She sees a bug, stalks it like a hunter on safari, then, when she gets close, tosses the bowl over it like a Frisbee until she traps it, then secures the bowl to the floor with roughly three rolls of the finest strapping tape known to man. Then waits for it to die. Then waits for her dad to eventually come home and flush it. The Stepping on It with Your Shoe System of pest removal that has been the accepted worldwide practice for over two thousand years was, obviously, in need of a refresh. Katie saw an opportunity and seized it. Caroline saw the opportunity to continue pursuing her lifelong hobby of collecting empty boxes. She likes to display her empty box collection all throughout the house. There's the empty cracker box in the pantry. The empty Toaster Strudel box in the freezer. The empty Trix box in the bathtub. Like Picasso's art being displayed on the walls of the MOMA, Caroline's work can be seen in the finest cupboards, tables, floors, shelves, dishwashers, dryers, car floorboards, bed sheets, and that little nook between the bathroom wall and the bottom of the toilet tank at her museum called home. And 2011 is also the year Kelly got a job and moved out of her college apartment in San Marcos, Texas, to Richmond, Virginia, to pursue a career as a producer of television commercials. Kevin asks you, dear reader, to please help settle a bet. What do the words "Please be completely packed by eleven a.m. and ready to leave by one in the afternoon because we have twenty-seven hours of driving ahead of us in a crappy U-Haul" mean? Is it (A) Please be completely packed by 11:00 a.m. and ready to leave by 1:00 p.m. because we have twenty-seven hours of driving ahead of us in a crappy U-Haul. Or (B) Please have absolutely nothing packed when your father arrives at 11:00 a.m. in a crappy U-Haul, and in fact not even have any boxes for packing, and then spend the entire day hanging out with friends and saying good-bye, and leave all the packing to your dad and then get mad at him when he wraps all your dishes and glassware in your fancy two-hundred-dollar sweaters, and then not be ready to leave until after 7:00 p.m., even though you have twenty-seven hours of driving ahead of you in a crappy U-Haul. Kelly chose (B). At Thanksgiving, Katie sensed Kelly being even more Kellyish than usual. "What is it you want, Kelly?" Katie asked her. *"I'm a woman,"* Kelly replied. *"The only way to answer that is, 'everything.'"* Moments later, they were deep into a scintillating discussion about guys with butt chins. Ah, college, what wonders you have worked upon Kelly. Also, 2011 is the year Julie moved back home, in January, in preparation to start grad school in August. But in the meantime, she got a job as a speech therapist for underprivileged Hispanic kids. She has taught Ellen many

Spanish words and phrases as well. *Perro* means "dog" in Spanish. *Orina de perro* means "dog pee." And *orina de perro en el suelo y en la manta y por todas portes pero de la hierba* means "dog pee on the floor and on the rug and pretty much everywhere but the grass." We tell you this because Julie brought home a dog she got from a Peruvian family who was so fed up with their stubborn puppy they gave it away. So now Kevin and Ellen have Beth's incontinent cat and Julie's drunken sailor dog. Kevin told Ellen he can't wait until Beth and Julie get houses of their own. "Congratulations, girls, here's your housewarming gift. A big bag of urine." (At an average temperature of 98.6 degrees, urine will, as a matter of record, actually heat a house.) As was alluded to earlier, 2011 is also the year Ellen turned fifty. She has asked that nothing be mentioned about her turning fifty, so this letter will dutifully comply. Ellen, being half a hundred, is happy to announce that 2011 is also the year Beth got engaged to a guy named Tyler. The wedding takes place in April. The bloodletting of Kevin is taking place immediately. He describes it like this: Imagine buying a brand-new Lexus. You love that shiny new Lexus. You love it so much that you drive that Lexus off the lot and then head straight for the nearest cliff, and just before you get to the edge of the cliff you jump out, and then you watch that Lexus hurtle off the cliff and explode down below into a fiery ball of fiery fire and you say, "Good-bye, Lexus." Kevin will eventually buy five Lexuses. In a totally related story, 2011 is also the year Kevin's misery was immortalized for everyone else's amusement in a GEICO commercial, courtesy of his friend Wade Alger, who wrote it. Perhaps you have heard it on the radio. It is the story of a sad-sack (but brutally handsome) father of five daughters who so desperately needs to find ways to save money that he makes all five of his daughters wait to get married in one large, group ceremony. If only life imitated art. If only Kelly found a guy to marry her. If only one could see how brutally handsome that actor was who portrayed Kevin on the radio. This is also the year Kevin discovered perhaps the one good thing about having all daughters. You can safely send them to Penn State, secured in the knowledge that nobody there will touch them. So that was 2011 in the Sutton household. Hell week, times fifty-two. Katie is fifteen, learning to drive, learning pest control, and learning that if you take a corner at too high a speed and too sharp an angle, automotive sheet metal is susceptible to unnatural laws of bending. Caroline is seventeen, a senior, still dancing, still pitching on her varsity softball team, still not pitching in to pick up objects like discarded clothing, used towels, dirty socks, other footwear not currently in use, half-eaten food, empty wrappers, hairbrushes, toothbrushes, nail-polish brushes, makeup brushes, paintbrushes, and animals that have made homes in the brush piles that have formed on her bedroom floor. Julie is twenty-two, going to grad school, conveniently leaving for class every morning and "not noticing" the pool of pee her dog Lima so thoughtfully left for Ellen and Kevin to sop up. Kelly is also twenty-two, and is desperately hoping her dad won't notice he forgot to take her off his AT&T phone plan and start making her pay her own way in this world. Beth is twenty-five and sending her dad Lexus brochures. And this letter must end now because Lima is peeing on the rug. *Dios mío*. That means, "Who ordered the urination machine?" in Spanish.

Merry Christmas and Happy New Year. From Kevin, Ellen, Beth,* Julie, Kelly, Caroline, and Katie Sutton.

*As of April 2012, Beth will no longer be licensed to use the Sutton name.

2012

Ellen is pregnant once again.

There is an old Lithuanian expression, "eating the goat to get to the bear," whereby you knowingly deliver one piece of news (the goat) that is so shockingly shocking, yet untrue, in order to ease the acceptance of what is actually an even more shocking, but true, bombshell (the bear) you really intended to drop, but don't want to come right out with in the first place because that even-more-explosive percussion of news, if delivered cold to an unsuspecting and un-pre-shocked world, would in fact be met with widespread hysteria, instant death-inducing heart attacks, and, in many cases, OMGs with multiple exclamation points. Now that you are properly desensitized, the Sutton family's shocking news for 2012 is, in fact, this: Caroline graduated from high school. Please, sit, take a moment to regain your bearings, and let your heart rate slow again before moving on. Yes, it's true, just nine short years after becoming a freshman, fourth-year senior Caroline Sutton actually graduated from high school. Kevin and Ellen have the transcripts to prove it. And, according to legal counsel, which has been consulted on multiple occasions just to double-check, the State of Texas cannot rescind it. Kevin and Ellen are proud to say, Caroline graduated second in her class. It was a long, difficult journey to get her there—wait a minute, did we say second in her class? We meant, in her *row*. Caroline graduated second in her row. Alphabetically. Row eighteen, seat two from the aisle, right next to a girl whose last name started with S-U-T-H. Following in the Tory Burch-shod footsteps of her older sisters, Caroline decided to bleed her parents dry. By going to college. Out of state. Ah, but Kevin and Ellen wondered, what college would accept a student whose grades were so, shall we say, remarkably unremarkable? When all else fails, there's always the SEC, where football is king and SAT stands for the day of the week they play it. Caroline got accepted to MU, the University of Missouri. Now, here is what Kevin cannot understand, and spent a good portion of the three-day freshman orientation weekend in June questioning, to the dismay of Caroline and several university officials. It is called the University of Missouri. Should it not then be, logically, UM? Or U of M? Why do they call it MU? After all, the University of Texas is UT, not TU. Same with the University of Connecticut (UConn), and the University of Massachusetts (UMass), and UCLA. Even the University of Kentucky, which just introduced Spellin' and the twenty-four-letter alphabet to its core curriculum in 2011, has the common sense to call itself UK. After probing Caroline on the stupid stupidity of this most important issue for three straight days, asking her to explain it slightly fewer times than Caroline asked Kevin for money in her eighteen-year leeching career, Caroline had had enough. "Dad, let it go. It's called MU because that's the way it is. The University of Oklahoma is the same way, it's OU. Same as the University of Colorado. It's CU, not UC." That argument is, to Kevin, much like an incontinent homeless man. It doesn't hold water. *"Don't invoke the 'Fourth Stooge Theory' on me, Caroline,"* he said. *"Adding one piece of inane logic to an already illogical argument does not in any way validate that argument. Just as adding a fourth stooge to the Three Stooges would not somehow make them any funnier."* Caroline said she could not wait until she was actually in college and far, far away from home. A few months later, while being dropped off for college and taking a stroll across campus with her dad, Caroline noted, "This campus smells like pickles." *"I noticed that, too,"* Kevin replied. *"That's not one of my favorite odors."* "You can't be too pleased with the ones coming out of you, either, Dad." Kevin is happy to report that Caroline lives far, far away at MU, or the Stupiversity of Missouri. Kevin and Ellen recently saw a picture on Facebook of something they had never seen before. Caroline at a desk, studying. The other huge news in 2012 (aside from Ellen losing forty pounds and getting her figure back to the shape that led Kevin to get her into this mess in the first place), news which would have been what they call "above the fold" in any non-Caroline-graduating-from-high-school news year, is that Beth and Tyler got married in April, in Atlanta. Welcome to the family, Tyler. Sorry. The Royal Wedding in Great Britain cost the taxpayers of England sixty million dollars. Take away the thirty-five million dollars for Royal security, and the ten million dollars for retouching the Royal dental work in the wedding photos, and that's about what an American wedding costs these days. A few weeks after the wedding, Kevin and Ellen got the bill. They are screwed. Royally. When the minister asked Kevin at the altar, "Who gives this child away?" Kevin's response was, "Her mother and I. And the MasterCard Corporation." All in all, the day was wonderful, but the entire thing went by in a blur. Kevin recalls there were flowers he paid for, but he's not sure what kind. He thinks he wore a tux he paid for, but can't recall what it looked like. (He is pretty sure he wore pants, though.) There was food of some kind he paid for, at some sort of reception thing with people. He vaguely recalls dancing with a bride or someone wearing a white expensive thing, he thinks it was Beth or one of the twins, and doesn't remember the song they danced to. And he sort of recalls there was an open bar, but doesn't really remember anything about it other than the Gentleman Jack that the five-foot-eight-inch bartender named Luis from the Dominican Republic poured for him all afternoon into the French-bevel-cut tumbler glasses over four half-inch ice cubes chilled at twenty-eight degrees as a way to drown his sorrows about how much the wedding was costing him and how much he missed his daughter Beth. But who really remembers weddings, anyway? That's why there are photos. Very, very expensive photos. Also, 2012 was the year Julie moved out of Kevin and Ellen's house and into a house a few miles away with a couple of roommates. Having a child who lives in the same city is a new phenomenon for Kevin and Ellen. Their children usually move as many states away as possible. Almost immediately after Julie moved out, though, Kevin and Ellen started noticing random things missing. Silverware, cups, stereo speakers, coins, meat, meat by-products, Caroline. Kevin and Ellen thought they were imagining things until one day they went over to Julie's house. "Hey, there's our lawn chair." "Hey, our pots and pans." "Isn't that the picture frame we're missing?" "Look, our spatula. And our garage." Kevin and Ellen were seriously considering putting an airport scanner at their front door to stop this rash of thefts but, since Julie last visited, their front door is missing. Recently, Kevin had this conversation with Julie after a busy week of giving speech therapy to her young patients. "Things are hectic, Dad. I had four kids on Thursday." *"I had five kids every day, Julie."* "Yeah, but this is different. I have to give each of them therapy for half an hour." *"I gave mine therapy for eighteen years."* Julie, it seems, does not possess Kevin's finely honed sense of humor. She will, however, steal it when he's not looking. Kevin and Ellen did actually find one thing in their house that wasn't there before Julie moved out. Peace and quiet. Because now Katie is the only Sutton girl left at home. Now there is nobody there to fight with. Leaving home eventually might be hard for Katie, though. She has trouble with doors. In September, Katie had to bring apple pies to school for—who knows why?—Apple Pie class or something. Katie convinced Julie to bake her a couple of pies. Julie, of course, waited until late the night before, forcing Katie to have to drive to her house the next morning on the way to school to get them. Julie forgot about it, though, and left early for work. When nobody answered the door at Julie's house, Katie started to freak out. Apparently, she did not want to get an F in Pies. So she decided to try the back door. Since the back gate was locked, she jumped over the fence—landing smack-dab in the realization that it had rained hard the night before and she was now ankle deep in a thick puddle of mud where Julie's dog Lima digs (and mostly pees, but Kevin and Ellen didn't want to point that out at the time). Now she was late. And muddy. And pie-less. And pee-soaked. And stuck in Julie's backyard. Then she spotted it. The doggy door. The light bulb flicked on in Katie's head. Turns out, it was one of those lame energy-saving light bulbs that end up being dimmer than an Alaska governor. And it turns out, while Katie's sense of reasoning is dog-sized, her hips are a bit wider. She got stuck trying to go through the doggy door. Desperately, she tried prying herself out for about ten minutes. But she was not budging. She had wedged herself in there good and tight. Now panic set in. She started to cry. So Lima, being thirsty because the door to her water bowl outside was now blocked, started licking the tears off Katie's face. Which made Katie start shaking her head to fend off Lima. Which did the job of attracting Julie's roommate's dog to the fun. He started chewing on Katie's hair. What a fun rag doll! That was the last straw. Apparently, being helplessly attacked by dogs on the way to pick up pies for school has a certain effect on people. Like a mother lifting a car off her baby, Katie mustered the strength to wiggle her way through the door. Ripping her blouse and skirt and a good hunk of skin on a nail in the process. But she was finally free. And she was inside Julie's house. Running late, she grabbed the pies and was heading toward the front door when Julie's roommate came out of her bedroom and screamed bloody murder because there was a pie thief in her house. That caused Katie to drop one of the pies. Fifteen minutes later, bloody, muddy, urine-y, tattered, hair chewed by a mongrel, dog-slobber-infused mascara smeared all over her face, toting a half-busted pie and a fully busted ego, Katie showed up late to school. Schools hate it when you're late. Especially on Picture Day. Granted, Kelly didn't have a day as eventful as that in 2012, but she did have an eventful summer. In a three-month span in Richmond, Kelly suffered through an earthquake, a tornado, and a hurricane. Her poor car suffered a lot of damage—when Kelly foolishly let her roommate take it to the airport and she ran it into a wall. It was then that her roommate informed Kelly that she didn't have insurance. Kelly, it seems, has forgotten a thing or two Kevin and Ellen taught her growing up. So, to repeat, once again, Kelly, here are a few of Kevin's Important Rules to Live By: Never play leapfrog with a unicorn. Never go to a British dentist. Never judge a book by its cover, unless the cover says it's about teenaged vampires; then, realize it will suck. Never visit a proctologist with unusually long fingers. Never text and drive, unless you are already on your way to the morgue. Never ask a bald man if he's having a bad hair day. Never say "gimme some skin" in a leper colony. Never tell your cab driver to "just surprise me." Never wear a hat to a beheading; that's just rubbing it in. Never wear a fanny pack (this should be obvious). Never go cliff diving with a guy named Cliff; it's just too confusing. Never make small talk with a midget. Never swim right after you've eaten, especially if you've just eaten Mexican food. Never ask your father to pay for a wedding. Never beat a dead horse, unless you are racing against it, because if you can't beat a dead horse in a race that's pretty embarrassing. Never ask what's in kidney pie. Never tell a zombie he looks like death warmed over. Never play Rock-Paper-Scissors with Edward Scissorhands, unless you are Edward Rockhands or Edward Paperhands. Never trust a Mayan meteorologist. Never admit to anyone that you juggle for a living. Never play air guitar in an air a cappella band. Never take the easy way out, unless the hard door is locked. And never, ever, ever, ever, under any circumstances, let anyone else drive your car. Oh, and while we are at it, never tempt fate by joking about your wife being pregnant. Because, as has already been proven with Beth, Julie, Kelly, Caroline, and Katie, the Sperm Fairy can be a real bear.

One more rule to follow: do not forget to have a Merry Christmas and a Happy 2013. From the Suttons, or what's left of us. (Wait a minute, who stole the ink cartridge out of the printer? Julie! And, hy, what happnd to th lttr " " on th kyboard, it was just thr a scond ago, I swar? Juli!)

2013

La Cucaracha.

Kevin's phone rang. He didn't recognize the number but he answered it anyway; he had been awaiting a call from Scarlett Johansson. Perhaps this was it. "Hello?" A frantic voice on the other end shot out, "Mr. Sutton, this is Medical Center Hospital in Plano. Your daughter Julie was hit by a car. We're with her right now in ER. She was riding her bike and someone ran her over." The first thought that goes through any father's mind at a time like that is, naturally, *wait, she's not still on our insurance, is she?* The second thought is, *oh, my God, is she all right?* Kevin asked that very question. "Oh, my God, is she all right?" The lady on the other end of the phone replied, "The car ran over both of her legs but somehow she didn't break any bones. It's a miracle, really. She's okay." Just then, one more thought went through Kevin's mind: *Ahhh, lady, next time, you might want to lead off with the "she's okay" part first.* You know the old saying that at the end of the world the only living thing to survive will be cockroaches (and maybe Keith Richards) because, no matter how many times you step on a cockroach, it simply does not die? (Cockroaches seem to have more lives than cats, and are slightly more loveable.) Well, in 2013, scientists identified one other organism that will walk the face of the lonely decimated Earth (assuming for a moment Earth's end will be caused by decimation, perhaps from a Tea Party candidate in the White House, or more likely from Earthlings unwittingly getting a look at Lady Gaga's actual face—

please, for your own good, do not look directly into it). When the Earth does come to its tragic final moments (which for Cubs fans will probably be the day right before Game One of the World Series they finally make it into—say in the year 2217, or 2216 if their draft picks pan out sooner), joining the cockroach in its quest of indestructibility is Kevin and Ellen's own human cockroach, better known as their twenty-four-year-old daughter Julie. No matter how many times life stepped on Julie in 2013, she refused to die. Like the movie *Invincible,* Julie is invincible. Like the movie *Never Say Die,* Julie never said die. Like the movie *I Am A Speech Pathologist,* Julie is a speech pathologist. In 2013 Julie was 1) run over by a car while riding her bike, 2) driving on the highway when a ladder on the truck in front of her fell off and nearly crushed her car, 3) outside her house when her rug-peeing dog, Lima, was run over by a car, 4) on the highway when the car in front of her suddenly stopped and she plowed into it and she totaled her car, 5) driving in the mountains of Colorado when she hit a patch of ice and her car spun out of control and she stopped with her two front tires hanging off the edge of a cliff. Luckily, Julie walked away from it all (with only a scar on her leg). Luckily, Julie's dog lived to pee on another rug. Luckily, Julie wasn't on Kevin and Ellen's insurance. And, luckiest of all, she did this all before Obamacare kicked in. 2013 was a year of survival in the Sutton household. The oddest of things seemed to happen to the oddest of families. One day Katie inexplicably woke up with two pesos in her bed. What, is the Tooth Fairy Mexican? That explains why every time the kids lost a tooth, the landscaping looked awesome the next morning. One day Caroline discovered the driver's license of a female judge from Milwaukee in the back seat of her car. What's odd isn't that somehow the license of a female judge from Milwaukee ended up in the back seat of her car, it's that this woman was from Milwaukee and weighed less than four hundred pounds. Shocking. One day Julie got run over by a car. One day Kelly ate grasshoppers. She was in Mexico at the time. No explanation for why she ordered grasshoppers at a restaurant in Mexico was given. But, with Kelly, none was needed. Upon hearing Kelly ate grasshoppers in Mexico, Ellen responded, "Oh I wonder what the weather was like down there." One day Beth, who had to ride two hours each way to work in a ridesharing van every day, got into a fight with an angry Indian man named Harshit. (What would give a man named Harshit any reason to be angry?) Harshit flew into a blind mad rage an hour into the ride back home when the driver refused to turn the van around to retrieve the iPad he left at work. While the driver was cruising down the highway, Harshit actually attempted to take the keys out of the ignition so he would be forced to stop. Beth and the rest of the passengers wrestled with the guy as the driver of the van was flying at seventy-miles an hour down the highway trying to hang on to the steering wheel while Harshit tried to grab the keys. What a Bullshit move. (Bullshit is Harshit's older brother who pulled that same stunt back in India in the late 90s.) It took them about ten minutes to get Harshit to calm down and kindly take his seat, very very thanks. Beth retaliated the next day by going to 7-Eleven and filling her Big Gulp to the brim, taking an extra long sip from it, then filling it back up again, then taking another long sip, then refilling it to the brim and not paying for the extra Big Gulp she drank. That will teach India. (Sidenote: Harshit was fired from his job not long after for throwing a chair at his boss—perhaps in a heated dispute over Big Gulp revenues.) Poor Beth. Last year she married Tyler, and their wedding was overshadowed by the one-in-ten-trillion chance graduation of Caroline Sutton. Now, the year she and Tyler buy a house, that news is overshadowed by Julie inconsiderately getting run over by a car. Her sisters are so rude. Other acts of survival in 2013 included Kevin and Ellen surviving Katie's running commentary. Katie, on the state of Kevin's hairline: "Dad, you should become Jewish. A Yarmulke would cover up that bald spot perfectly." Katie, on having to find clothing for Nerd Day at school: "I hit the mother lode. I went into Mom's closet." Katie, on being invited to go out to eat with Kevin and Ellen: "Why would I want to have dinner with a couple of deadbeats?" Katie's text exchange with Kevin, as he landed back in Dallas from a trip to Mexico City and saw all the ice on the ground from the recent ice storm he had missed: "Katie, I thought I told you to get rid of all this ice before I got back." *"I am a daughter, not a sun."* Kevin and Ellen survived yet another college-visit tour, this time with Katie. To say that all colleges are pretty much the same would be an understatement. Kevin would like to invite you to take the following quiz. These are the actual slogans used by colleges they visited. See if you can pick out which college is which: College A: A tradition of excellence. College B: A legacy of excellence. College C: A legacy of tradition. College D: Excellence is our legacy and tradition. College E: We play football. So that was 2013 with the Suttons. Survival. Beth is twenty-seven and has a new job where she no longer has to spend four hours a day in a van commuting with a guy named Harshit. She and Tyler bought their first house in Atlanta. The first thing Tyler got for that house was a Kegerator. Kevin knew there was something he liked about that guy the minute he met him. Julie graduated from grad school this year, and is teaching speech pathology to Hispanic kids. And is alive after being run over by a car. Kelly is twenty-four and living in Richmond, producing TV commercials, and still producing requests to her dad for large sums of money. A conversation over Thanksgiving went like this: "Dad, I am going to buy a new car. How much can you kick in for it?" *"How about a hundred thousand dollars?"* "Really!? I was just thinking about getting a small used car." *"Keep thinking that way."* "But with a hundred thousand dollars, I could get a really nice car." *"Oh, I'm not giving you that money now. That's the money I already kicked in so you could get a college degree so you could get a job so you could start earning money so you could buy your own car."* Kelly bought her own car. Caroline is nineteen and in her second year at Missouri and somehow has a B+ average. That is not a typo, sorry if your heart stopped. She asked if she could study abroad next year. Kevin told her not to waste the money. He has been studying six broads for more than thirty years and he has yet to learn a darn thing. Katie is seventeen and a senior in high school. Which means, finally, after surviving twenty-two straight years of Meet The Teacher nights, Kevin and Ellen went to their final one ever in 2013. They were informed that, this year, Katie's class is going to dissect cats. Knowing how financially strapped the Richardson School System is, Kevin, ever the humanitarian, generously offered up their two cats. For science. And to help the school's budget. Unfortunately for Kevin, the cats survived the offer. Not even science wanted them. The Sutton cats, like cockroaches, and Julie, have a lot of staying power.

Merry Christmas, and a less odd 2014, from Kevin and Ellen and the rest of the Sutton girls—those who are living with us, those who are living away from us, and those who, we are happy to report, are still living after being run over by a car.

AND IN CONCLUSION

So, as I wrap up my résumé, in closing I would just like to say, thank you for considering me for a position as director of Midol's Research and Development Department.

As you have seen, from my extensive experience raising five daughters, I know a thing or two about women. No candidate is better qualified. Because no man is more beaten down.

I look forward to hearing from you soon. Please, dear God, by next Thursday.

Sincerely,
Kevin Sutton

P.S. If, however, there are still any lingering doubts, I leave you with one last nugget of research.

A DOZEN THINGS YOU NEVER WANT TO HEAR YOUR TEENAGE DAUGHTER SAY

1. We're naming him after you, Dad.
2. What do you think it costs to remove a tattoo?
3. We have insurance, right?
4. He's not going to school; he wants to be a DJ.
5. Let's get another cat.
6. I want to go to college.
7. Wouldn't it be cool if Mom and Dad had another kid?
8. My stage name is Cinnamon.
9. Goth.
10. Let's listen to rap and/or hip-hop.
11. Breasts are coupons for free stuff.
12. Now we're orphans.

ABOUT THE AUTHOR

Kevin Sutton has written hundreds of essays, letters, pamphlets, leaflets, handbills, circulars, and books on raising daughters, and is considered one of the world's foremost experts on child rearing.

Childless, he lives alone in Malibu, California, with his sixteen cats.

Made in the USA
Lexington, KY
06 August 2016